Sing the Sun Up

Sing the Sun Up

Creative Writing Ideas from African American Literature

Edited by Lorenzo Thomas

Teachers & Writers Collaborative

New York

Sing the Sun Up: Creative Writing Ideas from African American Literature

Library of Congress Cataloging-in-Publication Data

Sing the sun up : creative writing ideas from African American literature /
    edited by Lorenzo Thomas
            p.   cm.
  Includes bibliographic references (p.   ).
  ISBN 0-915924-54-4 (pbk. : alk. paper)
1. African literature--Afro-American authors--Study and teaching.
2. Afro-Americans in literature--Study and teaching. 3. Afro
-American students--Education--Language arts. 4. Interdisciplinary
approach in education. 5. American literature--African influences.
6. Creative writing--Study and teaching. 7. Afro-Americans--
Authorship. I. Thomas, Lorenzo, 1944–   .
PS153.N5B557   1998
810.9'896073'07--dc21   97-42310
                                                  CIP

Teachers & Writers Collaborative
5 Union Square West
New York, N.Y. 10003-3306

Cover and page design: Christopher Edgar.

Front cover image:

LAWRENCE, Jacob.
"The migration gained in momentum." Panel 18 from *The Migration Series*. (1940–41; text and title revised by the artist, 1993). Tempera on gesso on composition board, 18 x 12" (45.7 x 30.5 cm). The Museum of Modern Art, New York. Gift of Mrs. David M. Levy. Photograph © 1997 The Museum of Modern Art, New York.

Printed by Philmark Lithographics, New York, N.Y.

Acknowledgments

This publication was made possible, in part, through support from the Lannan Foundation and the NEA Challenge Grant Program.

Teachers & Writers programs are made possible, in part, through support from the National Endowment for the Arts, the New York State Council on the Arts, and the New York City Department of Cultural Affairs.

T&W also thanks the following foundations, corporations, and individual donors: Anonymous Donor, Apple Computer, Inc., Bell Atlantic Foundation, Bertelsmann USA, The Bingham Trust, Booth Ferris Foundation, Bronx Borough President and City Council, The Bydale Foundation, The Louis Calder Foundation, The Chase Manhattan Foundation, Consolidated Edison, Simon and Eve Colin Foundation, Charles E. Culpeper Foundation, Heavy D and the Universal Music Group, Marvin Hoffman and Rosellen Brown, J. M. Kaplan Fund, Morgan Stanley Foundation, M&O Foundation, Manhattan Borough President and City Council, National Broadcasting Company, Inc., The New World Foundation, New York Times Company Foundation, Henry Nias Foundation, Overbrook Foundation, Thomas Phillips and Jane Moore Johnson Foundation, Prudential Foundation, Queens Borough President and City Council, Maurice R. Robinson Fund, Helena Rubinstein Foundation, the Scherman Foundation, Steven Schrader and Lucy Kostelanetz, and T&W's many individual members.

For Rochelle Lang

Table of Contents

OTHER POSSIBILITIES

Preface

by Lorenzo Thomas

TO DEMONSTRATE that black writers have made great and lasting contributions to American literature requires no strenuous effort. One may simply mention James Baldwin and Toni Morrison, Lorraine Hansberry and Langston Hughes, and the case is made. It is also true, however, that African American writers are still subject to a kind of intellectual segregation. While some may enjoy the celebrity that comes from appearing on bestseller lists or television talk shows, their works often remain strangers to our classrooms. Perhaps—usually in February for Black History Month—a teacher will offer a page from Paul Laurence Dunbar; perhaps a student will recycle her Sunday School recitation of James Weldon Johnson's "The Creation" for extra credit. And that, unfortunately is sometimes as far as it goes.

While it is true that the content of much African American writing is the necessary retelling of an epic story of survival and struggle, too often one finds that this literature is introduced into the classroom purely for its sociological significance. The result is the mistaken impression that the literature has no relevance beyond this one dimension. How often, for example, do we discuss how cleverly—and artfully—the poems of Langston Hughes combine free verse rhythms and rhyme, managing to mingle the simplicity of Imagism with the complex "signifying" of African American speech?

In fact, the works created by African American writers comprise a rich and marvelously diverse treasure for open-minded readers and aspiring writers.

From Phillis Wheatley's neoclassical elegies of the 1770s to the present, black poets have always demonstrated their ability to produce excellent work in traditional or contemporary idioms. As Countee Cullen, himself a master of the sonnet form, wrote in 1927, "since theirs is also the heritage of the English language, their work will not present any serious aberration from the poetic tendencies of their times." What Cullen did not say, however, is that African American writers—from Jean Toomer to Ishmael Reed—have just as often been in the vanguard of stylistic innovation and literary experimentation.

Though black writers often present the unique perspective that comes from the experience of living in a society that is often hostile to their blackness, African American literature can hardly be called "exotic." It is a literature grounded in the experiences and the languages of the New World, and any reader who explores American literatures in English, Spanish, Portuguese, or French will find the expressive voices of Africa's children.

It should be clear, though, that we are not talking about a culture that is separate and distinct. This is apparent even in a work like Dudley Randall's *A Capsule Course in Black Poetry Writing*. Published in 1975, this little book is a collaboration by Randall, Gwendolyn Brooks, and Haki R. Madhubuti (then known as Don L. Lee). While Madhubuti exhorts young African American writers to be black and proud of their heritage, Randall's sound and useful advice for beginning writers differs very little from that offered by rigorous defenders of traditional craftsmanship. Indeed, both Randall and Brooks urge the aspiring poet to read widely and to experiment with various forms until he or she has mastered them. Like Countee Cullen, these three mentors of the Black Arts Movement felt that aspiring writers should learn the *techniques* of their craft. And, even in the militant mood of that era, it was certain that the craft of the sonnet is as beautifully evident in the works of Cullen and Claude McKay as it is in the poems of Keats that *they* studied. McKay, however, expands our literary range; his poem "If We Must Die" (1919) established the sonnet as a vehicle for political protest in a way that no previous poet of the English language had imagined. In short, works by African American writers offer a complete inventory of poetry's myriad possibilities.

In this collection, distinguished authors and gifted teachers share tested techniques and professional insights, demonstrating how the rich resources of African American literature can be made accessible to readers of all ages and backgrounds; how these works can illuminate real-life experiences or enhance the type of deep imaginative engagement that used to be known, and treasured, as vicarious experience; and how—as models—these works can be useful to beginning readers and writers or introduce more sophisticated writers to excitingly innovative approaches to understanding and crafting language. By presenting examples of effective literary models and student writing, standard compositional methods and poetic devices come alive in this book. It is the difference between the list of ingredients and directions that one finds in recipes, and the delight of a welcome table laden with an array of colorful and inviting dishes.

Poet-teacher Opal Palmer Adisa, in her essay "Sticks and Stones," uses works by Countee Cullen and others to show how the particularity of an incident that moves a poet to write can, in fact, communicate on a "universal" level. Phillip Lopate, Julie Patton, Michael Morse, Elizabeth Raby, and Renée-Noelle Felice examine new ways to make the works of major writers such as James Baldwin, Jean Toomer, Margaret Walker, Etheridge Knight, and Nikki Giovanni useful to elementary, high school, and college students. I've also included my account of using Nobel laureate Derek Walcott's work in an adult poetry workshop.

Our focus is not entirely on using works that are strictly "literary," however. Kent Alexander suggests that African American folktales can be a valuable starting point for playwriting workshops, while Ilise Benun and Susan Marie Swanson point our attention to materials that can be effective resources in working with very young readers.

During the 1960s, a distinctive style of literary expression was developed by writers associated with the Black Arts Movement. Intended to reach an audience of "everyday people," this work was colloquial, improvisational, and meant to be read aloud. The writers generally looked to jazz and rhythm and blues as models. In 1972, Howard University professor Stephen E. Henderson presented the first major study of this type of work in his book *Understanding the New Black Poetry*. As Henderson pointed out, African American vernacular speech—with its subtle and complex use of humor and irony—has provided a rich vein of linguistic ore that has been profitably mined by black writers and orators. Scholars have shown that some of this language play is related to the same African sources that inform spirituals, the blues, and the improvisational structure of jazz.

Aspects of this oral tradition in African American poetry are addressed in this volume in essays by Len Roberts, Janice Lowe, Aurelia Lucía Henriquez, and Melba Joyce Boyd. In addition to examining contemporary practitioners of this "sound science" such as Jayne Cortez, these essays also direct attention to poets such as Langston Hughes and Puerto Rico's Luis Pales Matos, both pioneers in the literary adaptation of creolized vernacular speech in the 1920s. As Mark Statman also shows in his essay on Cortez and Lucille Clifton, there are many types of eloquence and many ways of approaching the crucial question Keats raised in "Ode on a Grecian Urn."

The final group of essays explores a number of intriguing topics. Ron Padgett offers a fresh look at the surrealism of Aimé Césaire, while Peggy Garrison shows how Rita Dove's work lends itself to exercises in creating point of view. Catherine Barnett develops a fine approach to teaching personification from Zora Neale Hurston's folk-based expression, and Patricia Spears Jones notes how African American writers fit into the more experimental zones of contemporary literature. Finally, and most appropriately, Margot Fortunato Galt's essay, "The Great Migration," outlines ways for writing teachers to draw upon other art forms and history, reminding us that writing must always "be as real as things are."

Not long ago, as debates about "political correctness" raged across the land, wearing T-shirts with purposely offensive slogans became the fad. One of the silliest ones declared IT'S A BLACK THING—YOU WOULDN'T UNDERSTAND.

Don't you believe it.

The eloquent and passionate message of 250 years of African American literature—and the purpose of the book you now hold in your hands—is affirmation of the fact that the goal of every writer is to *communicate*, to come face to face with your own most profoundly true experiences, and to find the art and words to make the whole world understand.

Opal Palmer Adisa

Sticks and Stones and Words As Weapons

What African American Poetry Teaches Us

THE EXTRAORDINARY DIFFICULTY of childhood, as I recall it, is making sense of an often contradictory and unpredictable world handed down by adults. Adults offer children maxims meant to buffer and protect, but sometimes these maxims do not help, leaving children with nowhere to vent their frustrations, voice their fears, or solicit other help to decipher an incongruent world. This condition of the child in some ways seems to parallel the experience of African people in the diaspora: that of a people taught one set of rules that often does not apply to them, or are made to pledge allegiance to a country that has repeatedly discriminated and alienated them. Because of this there are chants and charms, mantras and prayers to help others regain their balance and move forward. African American poetry disproves the notion that words can't hurt us. While some words hurt and maim and disfigure, other words heal, nourish the soul, salve the will, and strengthen the determination.

When I was a child my mother often told me the saying, "Sticks and stones can break your bones, but words can never hurt you." In truth, however, words often cut me to the bone, caused me to falter, to doubt myself, prompted tears, and left me bruised and wounded. I remember particularly one incident in which my friend Trevor and I had a quarrel over some marbles and he shouted at me, "Is bad-mind, you bad-mind 'cause you don't have any father." Because my parents were divorced before I was five, I saw my father infrequently, mostly during the summer months. Before I could rejoin, "Of course I have a father even though he doesn't live with me," tears blinded my eyes and smothered my voice. When my mother told me that Trevor did not know what he was talking about, it did not console me. Had Trevor hit me and tried to grab the marbles I had won from him, we would have fought, but then I think we would have resumed our friendship fairly quickly. However, I never felt I could quite trust him after that and so our friendship had a quick death. I never again allowed him close, not knowing what other words he would hurl at me.

Perhaps that is why I was instantly drawn to Countee Cullen's "Incident" the first time I read it, not only because the poem is so well crafted but because of the incident with Trevor. Cullen's poem, as well as other writings by many African American authors, eliminates the fluff and gets right to the heart of the matter:

Incident

For Eric Walrond

Once riding in old Baltimore,
Heart-filled, head-filled with glee.
I saw a Baltimorean
Keep looking straight at me.

Now I was eight and very small,
And he was no whit bigger,
And so I smiled, but he poked out
His tongue, and called me, "Nigger."

I saw the whole of Baltimore
From May until December;
Of all the things that happened there
That's all that I remember.

Especially with poetry, my approach to teaching is visceral. I never teach what I don't like. I teach what I love, what I believe to be good writing, but mostly, I teach pieces that have integrity, that speak from a place of intimacy, pieces that provide another point of view, and even offer a path that others might travel. Of course, I mention that the poets are African American and that the poems refer to a specific social era, but I also stress that a good poem transcends the boundaries of a set historical time-frame.

I began one of my residencies with the tenth grade students from Oakland High School Visual Arts Academy and their teacher Judi Yeager, by writing in bold letters on the board, "STICKS AND STONES MAY BREAK YOUR BONES, BUT WORDS CAN NEVER HURT

YOU!" The students were predominately Asian, with some African Americans, Chicanos, Latinos, and Euro-Americans. The students were familiar with the maxim, but like me, most did not believe it. Many had anecdotes to illustrate just the opposite. They all agreed that words hurt, and we went around the room identifying words such as *death, ugly,* and *stupid* that did in fact hurt people very badly. Next, I gave them all a xeroxed sheet of Cullen's poem "Incident"and asked for a volunteer to read it aloud. Afterwards we analyzed it line by line to discern how Cullen develops the poem, and how the poem affects the reader. The narrator of the poem never says he is hurt, but his sadness is evident. Then, I had students reflect back to when they were between six and ten years old, to see if they could recall a memory of when someone said something that hurt them. For most of them, the hurtful words were from strangers, so they identified very strongly with the boy in the Cullen poem. After discussing the poem, we read Langston Hughes's "Dream Deferred" and "Freedom." I discussed how Hughes uses rhetorical form to begin and close "Dream Deferred," and how that makes the poem open-ended, yet conclusive. Although the first and last lines of the poem are phrased as questions, the inference is that the answers are obvious. Therefore the questions turn in on themselves and can (and should be) read as statements. The accessibility of the poem provides me with the opportunity to discuss the use of concrete, specific language such as, "Does it stink like rotten meat?" that is graphic. All the students could relate to this poem; some of the Southeast Asian students talked about how for some of their families, the American dream seemed elusive, if not totally impossible.

From the Langston Hughes poems, I moved to the piercing irony of Frank Marshall Davis's succinct poems, "Giles Johnson, Ph.D." and "Robert Whitmore":

Giles Johnson, Ph.D.

Giles Johnson
had four college degrees
knew the whyfore of this
the wherefore of that
could orate in Latin
or cuss in Greek
and, having learned such things

he dies of starvation
because he wouldn't teach
and he couldn't porter.

Robert Whitmore

Having attained success in business
possessing three cars
one wife and two mistresses
a home and furniture
talked of by the town
and thrice ruler of the local Elks
Robert Whitmore
dies of apoplexy
when a stranger from Georgia
mistook him
for a former Macon waiter.

After two students read the poems aloud, I asked the group to consider the poems' titles. Why the personal names? What did Davis want to impress upon the reader? The students replied astutely that these poems were about real people, and that by titling them by the name, pseudonyms notwithstanding, Marshall heightened the poem's credibility. I detected that much of the irony was lost on the students, even the African American students, who failed to discern that Frank Marshall Davis was not necessarily writing from a place of sympathy. Davis's simple use of "because" in the second to last line of "Giles Johnson, Ph.D." is a jab at the ludicrousness of this educated man, whose education led to his downfall because he somehow believed that education would be a buffer against racism. Similarly, Robert Whitmore died of apoplexy because his success did not distinguish him above the status of a Macon waiter. Here Davis is revealing how some successful African Americans lose touch with the fact that regardless of their success, they are still living in a very color-conscious society. The students had no trouble understanding this phenomenon.

Finally, we turned to Maya Angelou's "Still I Rise," which celebrates resilience. The students very much enjoyed the poem, especially the refrain, "I rise." This gave us yet another opportunity to discuss poetic techniques, such as repetition. In this case "I rise" is an affirmation that the narrator of the poem will indeed rise, and at the close of the poem, the truth of the refrain is confirmed. This poem is also a good example of how to use metaphor and to incorporate cultural and familial history into a poem. We also discussed rhyme and free verse. I cautioned students to refrain from rhyming if the content of the poem would suffer to accommodate a rhyme pattern.

After we read and discussed all the poems, the students reread them, selected the ones they related to most strongly, and wrote poems of their own, employing one or more of the poetic techniques we had discussed. The range of response was wide; below are six poems from that class.

In Mind

In the mind of a soul, and the weakness of death
The truth of a secret could be swept.
In a hidden sea, down deeply in the ocean,
no treasures keep, or the tides in motion.

In the mind of a soul, and the darkness of light,
the lies of a devil, and the hell of the night.
In a hollow cave, rough rocks and stones,
no hungry bears, nor the sound of tones.

In the mind of a soul, and the brightness of green,
Empty of seeds, which bare cannot be seen.
In a shivering cold, and the breeze of ice,
no motherhood that could bear us life.

—*Jessie Lu*

I Am Strong

I sit in my room and stare into space
I think to myself, I'm not going anyplace
As I hear footsteps coming from behind my back
I know that this will be an attack
I am strong
I am strong

As I look up to her, I can see through her eyes
That all she thinks of me are sorrows and cries
But still I would not let her see the weak side of me
I am strong, I have power, that's what I want to be

I am strong
I am strong

She repeatedly brings me down
I know it will not work because I will turn it all around
I will pull up, way up high
Show her that I'm not what she thinks
I'm someone that's strong, a big and great power
I'm someone with bright light, a strong high tower
I am strong
I am strong

  —Cuc Hui

Left in the Cold

In my mind,
You were willing to set me free,
I thought you were going to be there for me
Because I was only three.
You left Mom with sorrow,
And me with pain,
Why did you have to go?
Can you please explain?

Now I'm fifteen,
Do you understand why?
Are you an angel?
Will you ever say good-bye?

  —Mae Chi

China Boy

I am a Chinese Boy
Growing up in such a weird country,
A land with many races
And a language that sounds funny.

A land where people can vote
And kids can go to school,
Living in houses instead of boats
And yet to us, the culture is new.

In America I have the right to get an education
And be all I can be,
To the laws I pay attention
My future belongs to me!

Trying to fit in and act like Americans.
Taking on American names like Floyd or Troy,
But I will never forget my native language, culture, and religion
I am a Chinese Boy.

    —*Kuong Lu*

Star

Does it dry up like a raisin in the sun?
No!
Does it stand side by side?
Yes!
Or can you reach it
From the distance of the sky?
It can be reached by your heart.
Stars are hard to find.
Stars are bright.
Stars are shining.
Stars are here, so hold them tight.

—*Tim Nanphosy*

Don't Try to Get Me Down

Don't try to get me down!
Because . . .
The harder you push
the harder I'll stand.
Strong like a diamond.
I'll never fall!

Don't try to get me down!
Because . . .
I'm solid like a rock
and strong like Mike Tyson.

Don't try to get me down!
Because . . .
Soon I'll get tired

of being pushed around,
and before you know it
you'll be knocked out.

—*Blanca Baines*

Interestingly, the students didn't seem to care whether or not the poems were by African Americans. Those who were not African American were surprised at how applicable the poems were to their own lives.

› › ›

Later, I used the same poems with a combination fifth-sixth grade class at Burckhalter Elementary School. Many of the Burckhalter students live in a low-income area in Oakland that is plagued by violence. The students were predominantly African American; about a quarter were Southeast Asian. The idea of losing sight of one's dreams and vivid memories of numerous "incidents" dominated our discussion. We spent a long time discussing the Countee Cullen poem. Most chose to write about painful feelings and images that they had not shared with anyone. When I had students read their poems to the class, it was evident that these feelings had left an indelible mark on them. I can only hope that the opportunity to write about such traumas helped these young people to put some closure to their memories. However, as evident from several of the poems, not all of the major incidents in their young lives were negative; birth, for instance, continues to be a source of great joy and optimism for these children and their families.

Hit

I saw my sister get run over.
She flew in the air and hit
the ground.

I saw the ambulance
come and take her
away to the hospital.

The car was blue
the street was red
but she wasn't dead.

—*Lakesha Lacole Mackel*

That Special Day

Qiana Crawford
was born in
1984. It was
a glorious day.

When they had
me I was the
prettiest thing on my
block. When

I walked down
the street people
said, "Ow wee
your baby is

so pretty." Now
I'm grown
and they still
to this day
say, "Ow wee
you are so pretty!"

—Qiana Denice Crawford

A Time

There's a time for fun, a time to
play, every time, every day. Having a time
to see and watch TV, a time for basketball.

There's a time to kick it, a time to
just chill. There's a time for every
thing. There's a time for a party.

A time to be hardy, a time
to buy, a time to sigh. There's a
time to have fun, a time to play in the
sun and there's a time to rest.

—Robert Ellis

Baby Sister

On April 1983
all my attention went away.
My baby sister was born.
Next thing I knew I lost
my room I share with that
brat today.

The next thing I knew
I had to share that
room forever and ever.

After a few years my
attention came back
and everything was
better. But something
weird has happened now.
I love my baby sister.

> —*Tammie Clark*

Getting in a Fight

Getting in a fight
using all my might
also all my sight.

Getting home at night
saying it's alright
keeping myself warm.

Signing a form
at school in the
morning. Getting home at night

Keeping myself all tight
going to sleep and
not hearing a beep.

> —*Toan Bao Phu*

The Special Day

On a very cold night
a person entered our
world for the very
first time. This person
is special because she
is related to me.

My whole family was
happy in the USA and
across the Pacific.

She is my cousin
a beautiful baby and
a special day.

—*John Gallan*

I Wonder If She's Going to Die

I wonder if she's going to die.
My Auntie is very hurt.
She got shot three times,
once in her neck,
once in her arm,
and once in her stomach.
I wonder if she's going to die.
I had a dream that the devil
had taken her away
and I cried and cried
and then I woke up.
On Mother's Day she had
a high temperature.
It was one hundred and four.
I started to cry.
I said to myself
I wonder if she's going
to die.

—*Qwanisha Stokes*

Being Somebody

Don't let your life just drift away
standing on the corners
and drinking all day.

You want to be somebody
but do nothing to help.
You get put in jail
and wonder why all is hell.

All these people getting Ph.D.'s
while you're just chillin'
feelin the nice breeze.

You need to do something
with your life, thinking you're
all cool. Get an education and
go to school.

 —Chaner Jones

As a writer and teacher, I use African American literature with students at all levels, elementary through college, to explore their pains and joys without apology. It is an occasion to come together and share, spill guts, write, and help to cleanse the soul.

Sticks and stones and words cause pain for people who must constantly navigate through societies rife with contradictions. African American poets have taken the pain, simmered it, and transformed it into balm. That, it seems to me, is the greatest lesson that African American poetry teaches: how to heal.

PHILLIP LOPATE

Teaching James Baldwin

WHENEVER I HAVE USED personal essays to motivate students to write their own, I have relied on James Baldwin's work, because I know that he will get high school and college kids engaged and excited. The resistances they show to Lamb, Hazlitt, Montaigne, and all those other "old-timey writers" seem to melt away under Jimmy's fiery gaze. It is Baldwin to the rescue, in part because his honesty and passion are very attractive to young people; but also because Baldwin dramatized adolescence again and again as his own particular crucible of selfhood—boy preacher, loss of faith, yearnings to write, father's death, foregoing college, struggles over racial anger and sexual preference—and sympathized so warmly with the efforts of all youth to forge an identity.

In an essay entitled "They Can't Turn Back," on the desegregation of the schools in the South, he writes, parenthetically and characteristically, about the "really agonizing privacy of the very young. They are only beginning to realize that the world is difficult and dangerous, that they are, themselves, tormentingly complex and that the years that stretch before them promise to be more dangerous than the years that are behind. And they always seem to be wrestling, in a private chamber to which no grownup has access, with monumental decisions. Everyone laughs at himself once he has come through this storm, but it is borne in on me, suddenly, that it *is* a storm, a storm, moreover, that not everyone survives and through which no one comes unscathed. Decisions made at this time always seem—and, in fact, nearly always turn out to be—decisions that determine the course and quality of a life. I wonder for the first time what it can be like to be making, in the adolescent dark, such decisions at this generation of students has made."

This is catnip to the young.

I am being a bit ironic because, while I love Baldwin's writing, I sometimes feel that I have to exert counter-pressure to pry students from its appeal and exercise a little critical intelligence. Once they fall under the spell of his voice, they tend to buy into his whole analysis of race, politics, America—the bombastically prophetic, wrongheaded parts as well as the sensible. What they really buy into is his presentation of self as a wounded being: there can be no doubt that, in a talk-show culture that enshrines victimhood, Baldwin plays exceedingly well.

‣ ‣ ‣

When I teach Baldwin I focus on his essays, because I think he is a great essayist—indeed, the most important American one since the end of World War II—and only a so-so fiction writer. His long novels, *Another Country* and *Just above My Head*, now seem windy and unfocused; *Giovanni's Room*, precious. When there is enough time, I have occasionally assigned *Go Tell It on the Mountain*, which many consider his best, just to show how the same material (a Harlem adolescence) may be treated via both fiction and non-fiction. To my mind, this first novel of Baldwin's, atmospheric but clotted, cannot hold a candle to his infinitely more expressive personal essay, "Notes of a Native Son."

A twenty-page miracle, a masterpiece of compression, "Notes of a Native Son" seems to pour out in a white-heat of emotional prose, though it is everywhere artfully shaped. The portrait of his father, David Baldwin (whom he later learned was actually his stepfather), is a model of unsentimental ambivalence. Many students, encountering it for the first time, are shocked to see that one can actually tell such tales out of school. Baldwin's ferocious and fastidious candor liberates them to begin writing about the meanings of their parents' lives.

I generally focus on the following amazing paragraph:

> He was, I think, very handsome. I gather this from photographs and from my own memories of him, dressed in his Sunday best and on his way to preach a sermon somewhere, when I was little. Handsome, proud, and ingrown, "like a toenail," somebody said. But he looked to me, as I grew older, like pictures I had seen of African tribal chieftains: he really should have been naked, with warpaint on and barbaric mementos, standing among spears. He could be chilling in the pulpit and indescribably cruel in his personal life and he was certainly the most bitter man I have ever met; yet it must be said that there was something else in him, buried in him, which lent him his tremendous power and, even, a rather crushing charm. It had something to do with his blackness, I think—he was very black—with his blackness and his beauty, and with the fact that he knew

that he was black but did not know that he was beautiful. He claimed to be proud of his blackness but it had also been the cause of much humiliation and it had fixed bleak boundaries to his life. He was not a young man when we were growing up and he had already suffered many kinds of ruin; in his outrageously demanding and protective way he loved his children, who were black and menaced, like him; and all these things sometimes showed in his face when he tried, never to my knowledge with any success, to establish contact with any of us. When he took one of his children on his knee to play, the child always became fretful and began to cry; when he tried to help one of us with our homework the absolutely unabating tension which emanated from him caused our minds and our tongues to become paralyzed, so that he, scarcely knowing why, flew into a rage and the child, not knowing why, was punished. If it ever entered his head to bring a surprise home for his children, it was, almost unfailingly, the wrong surprise and even the big watermelons he often brought home on his back in the summertime led to the most appalling scenes. I do not remember, in all those years, that one of his children was ever glad to see him come home. From what I was able to gather of his early life, it seemed that this inability to establish contact with other people had always marked him and had been one of the things which had driven him out of New Orleans. There was something in him, therefore, groping and tentative, which was never expressed and which was buried with him. One saw it most clearly when he was facing new people and hoping to impress them. But he never did, not for long. We went from church to smaller and more improbable church, he found himself in less and less demand as a minister, and by the time he died none of his friends had come to see him in a long time. He had lived and died in an intolerable bitterness of spirit and it frightened me, as we drove him to the graveyard through these unquiet, ruined streets, to see how powerful and overflowing this bitterness could be and to realize this bitterness now was mine.

It's all there, in this paragraph, but it requires some unpacking: Baldwin's sheer love of language; his intoxication with adjectives and adverbs, at a time when others avoided them; his Biblical rhythms, oral-sermon repetitions and series syntax ("and . . . and"); his oxymorons ("crushing charm"); his witheringly undercutting use of subordinate clauses ("never to my knowledge with any success"); his anglicisms ("rather" or the impersonal pronoun "one"); his verbal arrows and pointers ("yet it must be said that," "therefore"); his ability to sustain an extremely long sentence without wearying or confusing the reader; his willingness to pull back from a specific detail and make a broader generalization; his balance between rejection and tenderness, between rage and forgiveness; his ennoblings and deflations, often in the same sentence; his detachment and grim humor; and finally, his generous move to identify with, show complicity with, the sin ("this bitterness") he had seemed to be indicting.

Baldwin's prose is a carefully crafted, highly mannered (in the best sense) performance, and some of what I do when I teach him is to draw attention to his techniques. Students tend to inhale powerful prose in an undifferentiated rush, and I want to slow them down. Of course I don't wish to dilute their human feeling for this person who has suffered and witnessed great suffering; but I want them to understand the mastery of language that Baldwin accomplished, because this is part of the positive side of the ledger that helped him survive—and may help them survive.

I ask them to write a portrait of their mother or father, and to reflect on how we take on the traits of our parents, for better or for worse. Or I ask them to write about some incidents in which anger got the better of them, or to consider in an essay the nature of bitterness. Or just write about their growing up. By the time they have finished reading "Notes of a Native Son," they have often gotten the point—the challenge to be as honest and personal as possible on the page—and don't need much specific prodding to be off and running.

I follow it with as many Baldwin essays as I can, because I find that he is one of those writers whom students are willing to be saturated by. The more they read him, the more comfortable they become with his strategic moves and range of interests, and the more he seems a friend. Ideally, I can assign as a text the fat, collected book of Baldwin non-fiction, *The Price of the Ticket*, though one can also get by in a pinch with the earlier, paperback collections such as *Nobody Knows My Name* and *The Fire Next Time*, which are still in print. I ask them to read such gems as "Equal in Paris" (a narrative vignette about his getting arrested), "Stranger in the Village" (a meditation on otherness and the expatriate experience), "The Harlem Ghetto" (just to show how fully formed a stylist he was at twenty), "Alas, Poor Richard" (a searching double portrait of Baldwin and his partriarchal mentor/rival, Richard Wright), "Sweet Lorraine" (about the playwright Lorraine Hansberry), and, of course, "The Fire Next Time."

This last, full-length essay has portions as great as anything Baldwin ever wrote. You may have to supply a certain amount of historical context for students (the mood of the Sixties, the Civil Rights movement, the Black Muslims, etc.), though I have found, on the whole, that they get it. A bigger problem is the one I alluded to earlier: when this ambitious conglomeration of an essay begins to fall apart, the rhetorical smoothness of Baldwin's writing may fool students into not even questioning his apocalyptic overkill (such as that if America doesn't support revolutions abroad and at home, it will be burned to the ground).

The full-length essays that Baldwin continued to write, such as "No Name in the Street" or "The Devil Finds Work," are fascinating to teach—partly because they have such wonders in them and partly because they don't really hold together. (It's salutary, I think, for students to realize that the structural problems of essay writing may be so daunting when the ante is raised that even a master of the form can get bogged down.) In one sense the long, long essay *was* Baldwin's form: it brought out relaxed, self-surprising passages in him that nothing else did. But in another sense, he never figured out how to pull it off artistically, how to tie up the loose ends or give it an inevitable shape. This may have as much to do with the essay form today as with any inadequacies on Baldwin's part.

There are lessons anyone attempting to write personal essays can learn from Baldwin. How to dramatize oneself, for instance. Most personal essays misfire because of the blandness of the narrative persona, but this was never a problem for James Baldwin: he could always project himself on paper as in the midst of some burning conflict or dire strait. He was a bit of an actor, which an essayist needs to be—willing and able to take on one mask or another.

Another of his admirable qualities was a self-reflective insight that let us into his thinking process. Six pages into "Alas, Poor Richard," we encounter this passage:

> I was far from imagining, when I agreed to write this memoir, that it should prove to be such a painful and difficult task. What, after all, can I really say about Richard . . . ? Everything founders in the sea of what might have been. We might have been friends, for example, but I cannot honestly say that we were. There might have been some way of avoiding

our quarrel, our rupture; I can only say that I failed to find it. The quarrel having occurred, perhaps there might have been a way to have become reconciled. I think, in fact, that I counted on this coming about in some mysterious, irrevocable way, the way a child dreams of winning, by means of some dazzling exploit, the love of his parents.

I began by implying that James Baldwin had in some ways been fixated on his adolescent crisis and had over-acted the part of the racial victim. But we see from this passage how incomplete my assessment was; for it demonstrates the worldy, sorrowful realism and willingness to take responsibility for one's fate that makes Baldwin, at his best, a hero of American maturity. Perhaps what finally makes him so attractive to young people is the way he epitomizes the process of becoming a man, without losing touch with, or falsifying, the part of himself that remains a very vulnerable boy.

Bibliography

Baldwin, James. *The Fire Next Time.* New York: Dell, 1985.

———. *Nobody Knows My Name.* New York: Dell, 1978.

———. *The Price of the Ticket.* New York: St. Martin's/Marek, 1985.

JULIE PATTON

Cane in the Classroom

Using Jean Toomer's Classic

SOME TEXTS resonate so deeply within us that we never forget their haunting spaces. So we read them again and again, to ourselves and to others. This is what I do with Jean Toomer's *Cane*. Published in 1923, *Cane* is a seed-book at the root of modern American poetics, memorable for its striking language and rich, sensual imagery, and its alternation of prose vignettes and poems.

> Oracular.
> Redolent of fermenting syrup,
> Purple of the dusk,
> Deep-rooted cane.

These lines from *Cane* describe the close connection between a people and their environment, people the color of *caramel, oak leaves on young trees, gold glowing,* and *dark purple ripened plums,* immersed in their environment in a manner reminiscent of Brueghel's peasants. This intermingling of ground and figure in *Cane* invites us to explore the relationship between humans and their environment, between language and place. Sugar cane forms the background of Toomer's text. His characters are steeped in cane, their lives tied to the slow motion grind of it, and rage at the boiling point:

> The scent of cane came from the copper pan and drenched the forest and
> the hill that sloped to the factory town, beneath its fragrance. It drenched
> the men in circle seated around the stove. Some of them chewed at the
> white stalks, but there was no need for them to, if all they wanted was to
> taste the cane.

Everyone breathes this air; it colors the speech, thickens the tongue, and extends the southern drawl.

Toomer's lush stream of consciousness pulls us into a particular time and place that surge with the rhythm of a people trying to get a foothold. In this sense, *Cane* echoes the African diaspora: "The dixie

19

pike has grown from a goat path in Africa." But Toomer focuses on another mass odyssey, that of black people to the big cities of the north. The reader is awash in this critical moment, the south-to-north migration of a group so held in limbo that contemporary African-American literature still holds this pattern between its teeth. The seasons and internal rhythms of the agrarian past comes through in the work of Toni Morrison, Alice Walker, Zora Neale Hurston, and Jamaica Kincaid. On the other hand, James Baldwin, Ishmael Reed, Paul Beatty, Richard Wright, Walter Mosley, and Ann Petry seem to be the gate-keepers of the urban. *Cane* mirrors the same dichotomy. The north frames a largely male domain, while the American south is associated with nature and the fecundity of women:

> And when the wind is in the south, soil of my homeland falls like a fertile shower upon the lean streets of the city.

In *Cane,* city and country, male and female, dawn and dusk, and black and white are a space apart, but Toomer makes it clear that each informs or resonates in the other. Some of my Harlem and South Bronx students trace a similarly alternating pattern. I can tell which ones hop-scotch between South Carolina and Manhattan, Mexico or Puerto Rico and the Bronx: traces of these places show up in their vocabularies.

I read *Cane* to my students to provoke the creative writing impulse in them, but I have another motive as well. Like Toomer, I view writing as a potential nature preserve for endangered voices. Toomer wanted to articulate a future for a world facing extinction. Decrying the devastation of the pastoral world and the folk culture that was tied to it, he scored his memories of them into *Cane* as if its pages were another kind of earth, a field of view for preserving that world. Yet *Cane* is not a nostalgic lament for the segregated, sharecropper South, with its painfully oppressive conditions; it is an affirmation of the historical, cultural, and spiritual significance of a nation at a pivotal point in its history, faced with escalating industrialization.

> Red soil and sweet-gum tree
> So scant of grass
> So prolifigate of pines
> Now just before an epoch's sun declines.

In the Toomer poem "Song of the Son," the "son of the soil" returns to remind "a song-lit race of slaves" about the roots he fears they'll lose in city streets:

Though late, O soil, it is not too late yet
To catch thy plaintive soul, leaving soon gone . . .

Cane's characters live in close contact with the land because they are tied to it, yoked to the earth they sweat over and till. The enforced cutting of cane in the sharecropper South left a deep mark, another incision branding the skin of the so-called children of Cain. In this book, plum-dark women hold forth against a blood-burning moon, people and earth re-figure themselves, change shapes in the dark. Life in *Cane* is not romantic or idealized. It is often oppressive, violent, and terrifying. People disappear under the cover of a darkness Toomer refuses to cloak his own identity in, as he insists on blurring the color lines, or "passing" in a world that *Cane's* dusk-colored Karintha would never be allowed access to: "Her skin is like dusk on the eastern horizon."

The blurring of borders in *Cane* echoes the dreamy edges that all poetry encourages: a migration of meaning, as in this poem by Michael Spann, a Harlem fourth grader, written in response to hearing passages from *Cane:*

I find the chains of my ancestors and the underground railroad
a stair of broken wood-stack of stairs . . .
this is how they got out.
A big clear hot sky. There is no moon or stars. It is black out.
We light candles. As you come from the doctor it gets dark.
It's time to go home.
You sing and count plump sheep to go to sleep and have a red wobbled
    dream.

Like Elegba, the Yoruba trickster god, Toomer is always at a crossroads. He is the writer as nomad, searching for a deeper, more oneiric place of being, outside the identifying labels attached to an uprooted people. He is hell-bent on making a place out of a non-place, enclosing a space to be. He backtracks over the same words, the same scenes, as if digging deeper to make a receptive space for others to live in, as well.

▸   ▸   ▸

People tend to read black literature for its sociological content and ignore its aesthetic achievement. Experts argue about which texts are most relevant to the black experience, which ones constitute an "authentic black experience" for children, and which authors should represent African America and which should not. Entire legacies are oversimplified, homogenized into sound-bytes everyone can chew on. (One such "expert" once informed me that the writing of many of my Harlem students wasn't "black enough.") I wrote about some related concerns in my teaching diary:

> *Hic sunt leones* ("Here there are lions") was the designation used by Renaissance cartographers to indicate unknown, unexplored, and unmapped corners of the world—the vanishing point they directed their imaginations toward. The contemporary "inner city" conjures up a similarly forbidding terrain, with high walls and monsters sitting at the portals. The graffiti on the walls are the disembodied voice of a culture, echoing the fragmentation and dissolution of a community. I know firsthand how language can carve up the city streets, dismember and disembody the *civitas*. I can recall when another designation first skirted the edges of the place I called home. The word *ghetto* hovered about our heads for years before finally settling down on them. I remember asking my mother what they called the turf she inhabited as a youth. She said, "Oh, they just called it 'the neighborhood.'"

But language can enable children to re-site themselves, to renew and enrich our *civitas*. In many ways, imaginative writing gives students the tools to root their lives in a different landscape of meaning and address, tools to challenge and complicate language.

In the classroom, I do not shy away from bringing in literature that is "above" or "beyond" my students, provided that it is charged and evocative. I read aloud to them, walking around the classroom, bearing down on specific words to instill a dreamy and sometimes mysterious atmosphere, going on Gaston Bachelard's assumption that "the best training for poets is achieved through reverie, which puts us in sympathy with words and with substances."

> O R A T O R S. Born one an I'll die one . . . Been shapin words t fit my soul. Never told y that before, did I? Thought I couldnt talk. I'll tell y. I've been shapin words; ah, but sometimes theyre beautiful and golden an have a taste that makes them fine t roll over with y tongue.

I read parts of *Cane* to my elementary school students for a variety of reasons: to steep them in listening, to call attention to Toomer's imaginative use of language, or simply to fill the room with startling images. Of course I skip over the earthier passages, but it doesn't matter, since I am not emphasizing narrative.

I jump-start one imaginative writing exercise by using my voice to highlight a vocabulary that will sensitize my students to their surroundings, seizing details in the passage that emphasize the fact that the city (in our case, New York) is also land:

> Through the cement floor her strong roots sink down. They spread under the asphalt streets. Dreaming, the streets roll over on their bellies, and suck their glossy health from them. Her strong roots sink down and spread under the river and disappear in blood lines that waver south. Her roots shoot down.

In reading *Cane* aloud, I project certain words the way a painter dabs on color. *Boll weevils, dew, knolls, dusk, cotton-stalks,* and *pines* dot the landscape. *Cane* is perfectly scored for the ear, and I read it as a background text before giving an imaginative writing exercise that simply focuses on the associations and meaning inherent in the sound of single words. We start with the familiar *clouds, flower, rain, tree, pigeon,* etc., then move on to *mountain, forest, river* (things that are absent from the city). I don't explain much, I simply urge my students to *listen* to each word, to *see* what it is trying to tell them through the sounds, and to *notice* the shape and feel of the word in their mouths. Some words have a music, an inner mystery or depth that attracts the students, and they fall into the mysterious words, spend a long time contemplating them. I also emphasize the idea that the world speaks and inscribes itself in myriad ways. The children count the ways—trees "tell us" the seasons, deer and birds leave tracks we can trace, rivers babble, and rain rains.

Contemplating a certain word as both noun and verb introduces students to the idea that houses *house* us, clouds *cloud,* and rain definitely *rains,* and this prepares them for a writing process that underscores the idea of movement in a particular word's journey; otherwise students often end up with static poems instead of complex, shifting ones. Because Toomer's characters are elusive, I read *Cane* beforehand to establish the groundwork for this sense of movement. In any case, the students approach the assignment with the imperative of listening to a given word and thinking about what it does or about its impact on their lives. *Cloud, dusk, fern, rose,* or *snow.*

When I was a child, the "doing" words in my reader, *Skip Along,* were particularly inspiring. *Run, skip, hop.* There was something compelling about the fact that we were bombarded with "doing" words while anchored to our seats. *Come here . . . See my . . . Look up* always pointed to the outside world. The interplay between those commands and my own imagination made me leap, and I eagerly anticipated going outside to do all the thrilling things watercolor children and lithographed animals were engaged in all day long. But, as a visiting writer, I don't bring in childhood readers, I bring in the literature that tumbles from my own shelves, even grown-ups' books such as *Cane.* I trust that the hop, skip, and jump of my students' minds can help span the distance. The following poems by third graders at Harlem's P.S. 30 are proof of their ability to do this:

A Herd of Stars

I am a star
I have talked to the sky
I've shaken hands with the sun
But I only come out at night
I shine through the windows of planes that fly by
I shine on the birds that flap their wings at night
How do I see such things?
I work my way through by shining
But how do I shine?
I am mixed in a herd of stars
At night
I see the rain or snow fall
I do not speak
But if you listen very closely
you will hear my mind
I can see through the moon when it passes through the sky
I don't see everything, I just remember

I can hear the balloon float in the air from a child's hand
I can hear the rain come across the soft clouds
I can hear the groundhog fighting its shadow
I can hear the deep sea waving
I can hear the cries when I am reading a poem

I can hear the worm wriggle across the ground
waiting for a chick to come and eat it
I can hear the snowflakes tugging on a tree
I can hear tiny creatures trying to find a home
I can hear the silence

    —Leonor Moody

Listen to the Mystery

Listen to
The voice of water when
The water splashes
          to put out a fire
Listen
to a loud roar of water putting out fire
Listen to the mystery
    that hasn't been solved yet
Listen
        to the voice of the river crying
because it is in the palm of my right hand
Listen to the voice of water
    crying because it is hot and on fire
Listen to the voice of a
pencil when it is losing its head for you
    to write on
When
the point of your pencil breaks
It tells you,
"Use another pencil,
I'm tired."

    —Jamal Johnson

Silent World

When I am dreaming
I hear darkness switching to daylight
I can't see the wind but I can hear it

I hear the sun rattling in the day and the
moon shining at night time
I can hear my bed when I am jumping on it

I can hear chalk writing on a chalkboard
I can hear the trees shake

I can hear the flag saying hello to me
I can hear the other countries get together
and chatter

I can hear God singing in the blue sky
He doesn't scream

He sings in a nice low voice just so
that I can hear him.

—*Jamal Johnson*

The Baby's Heart

Remember the shadows
of the sky
Think of the wonderful
things that happen to you
Listen to the cradle that rocks the baby's heart
Hold the soul
of the baby's cries
Recall all the things
that happen to you
Romantic evenings, suffering, pain,
sorrow and death
Listen to the call of the trees
when it rocks your heart
to sleep
The cradle that is still
rocking in the baby's heart
Listen, listen
closely to the baby's cries
Hear the wind speaking to the sun
saying sun, sun
Shine harder so I can melt but I am not really dead
But sun, O sun, keep on shining
so you and I can hear the melting sounds of me
Listen to the winds that blow
Melt the baby's
               heart away
He will cry, I will cry
But the sorrow never ends

So, wind, blow, O wind, blow
so softly that we can hear the baby's
heart melt away
So wind, wind,
Dear old wind,
blow that baby's heart away

  —*Robert Yates*

Why do you
come out

At night
You're yellow

and bumpy
at night

You, like
glass in the sky

Why do you come
down

You, like
part of the sun

Part and grow
a wishing star

Wish your way
home

Go your way the dark
bark moon

  —*José Sullivan*

The Rain Is Falling

Hear me
the earth

Hear me
and the rain

A star

that's talking

the rain
falling

and jumping
Stars

are combing
their hair

in light
and going
to sleep

I talk to the rain
and stars

The rain crashing
and singing

The earth moving and the sky
darkening.

— *Guillermo Colon*

> > >

I often use *Cane* in conjunction with another poet's work or to explore a particular theme. The dictionary defines cane as a "thin reed used for wickerwork or baskets," a perfect companion for Chilean poet Cecilia Vicuña's investigation into the weave as a metaphor for writing and the connections between things, which she highlights by interweaving her poems with photographs. Children are fascinated by Vicuña's sense of permission and fantasy. Her poetry is often about the connections between humans and nature, but her images resonate further than the usual sloganeering that children might encounter on Earth Day, because her images are drawn from everyday life. Like Toomer, Vicuña implies that nature has the potential to lead us back into a fuller communication with the world.

In Vicuña's *Unravelling Words and the Weaving of Water,* there is an arresting image of clay snakes on a New York City water hydrant that point the way back to the sea. Students are also intrigued by Vicuña's image of trees filled with white yarn. Yoking, tying, binding, stitching, darning, knotting, and weaving are all related to the very ins and outs of writing, the loop-ti-loops children go through as they explore the links between themselves and the world, so that a ball in their hands suggests the sun and other round things, and eyes resemble stars.

> My lifeless controller keys
> keep me intact to my
> big-headed man, the sky.
>
> —*David Kaczynski, seventh grade*

I sprinkle the blackboard with the above-mentioned "weaving" words that proliferate in Vicuña's text, as well as other words that suggest the process of binding. Eventually we get to *glue*, *tape*, and *staples*, as is evident in the following poem:

> I'm sticking to my mother like strange
> glue. I love my mother like
> hearts flying in the sky. Shiny
> sky. Beautiful flower. You can guess
> the most beautiful world.
>
> The most beautiful people. Black
> white, it's nothing. The color gray it's
> a beautiful color. I'm looking for a
> beautiful world.
>
> I grow crazy weaves in my hair. Hair, hair,
> no hair, hair looks like string I keep combining and
> attaching. Sew new world, night
> tie yellow rope looping along jump up
> yokes
>
> —*Brenda Villot, fourth grade*

Poetry such as Vicuña's leaves an impression that things touch and fuse in strange conjunctions, as Ta'Donna Nagle, a fourth grader, in Harlem spelled out:

> I will attach my legs
> to a rooster
> so it will know
> it becomes morning
> I will combine
> a piece of

the world to a head
See if you can
find the difference
of the most
needed
I can attach a
needle into
the live skin of a
goat see
if it will run
jump stop
and cry or
be crammed
if I jump from
Earth to Venus
and sew
them together
one will fly
one will
be forced by
gravity

This poem emphasizes acts of will, empowerment, and possibility that underscore the very roots of the word *poesis* ("to make"). Ta'Donna repeatedly states *I will* while exploring connections we don't usually assume in everyday life. Suddenly we have worlds that didn't exist before, heaven and earth bound and unbound through transcendent leaps of the imagination. Ta'Donna's classmate Sabrina Valcarel, a child with a bent for challenging boundaries and edges throughout the normal classroom day, uses words associated with sewing, in a way that makes things seem totally integrated:

There it was
a girl
named Ta'Donna
And she was
wearing a
woven shirt
my sister
has stitched
her head to
the bedspring
in my garden

the leaves are grown,
hide them
in a kite
my mother sewed
my head to
the wall
because I
was very bad
I had attached
my friend's heart
to my soul so
She won't
go nowhere

Seventh grader Brandon Pittman wrote this poem:

A Battle with Trees

My eyes
connecting to the beautiful sight
of the young woman before me
My hair
Woven together like a wool
Sweater
As tall as I am
I stand a battle with trees

In poetry, one can situate one unlikely thing next to another. Art accomodates the deviating paths, twists, and turns real life can't. The analogical curves and spirals of poetry counter the linear thinking that rules the classroom. In this sense, language is both a way of creating space and extending its margins.

Obviously, writing and reading go hand in hand, just as listening and spinning once did. I go from classroom to classroom just as the ancient storyteller went from village to village. In my imaginative writing workshops, I observe the same relationship between work rhythms and stories. The students spin their own "yarns" before or after my delivery of *Cane*. Walter Benjamin said that storytelling was never a job for the voice alone, that hands pick up the rhythm, and lace, thread, or pound it into the work. To me, writing is often about a recovery of lost human gestures. In my urban classrooms, the rhythm of the sewing needle is replaced by the rhythm of the pen, and "when the rhythm of work has seized [them], [they] listen to the tales in such a way that the gift of retelling them comes to [them] all by itself" (Benjamin).

The joy of reading *Cane* to children is ultimately about the art of repeating stories. Call and response—the dialogue continues as contemporary urban culture bears witness and testifies to the intimacy of the human voice and human gestures. Thousands of schoolchildren have opened their ears to the fresh cadence of writers in the schools, such as June Jordan, Kurt Lamkin, Victor Hernández Cruz, Bernadette Mayer, Ron Padgett, Pedro Pietri, Grace Paley, Abiodun Oyewole, Wayne Providence, Janice Lowe, and others performing work that shores up distant voices in a new landscape of meaning. In *Cane,* many of my students hear speech rhythms that are akin to their own. Somewhere, inside the words, there's a pine-torched night punctuated by cries, yells, and whimpers that recall the voices of holy rollers or a wailing blues song. My reading of *Cane* emphasizes this sense of echo.

> Their voices rise . . . the pine trees are guitars,
> Strumming, pine needles fall like sheets of rain . . .
> Their voices rise . . . the chorus of cane

The alternation of prose and poetry and the persistent references to pine knots in *Cane* echo the culture of harvesting rituals:

> O Negro slaves, dark purple ripened plums
> Squeezed and bursting in the pine-wood air

> Pour O pour that parting soul in song,
> O pour it in the sawdust glow of night,
> Into the velvet pine-smoke air to night
> And let the valley carry it along

The lyrical patterns of *Cane* still reverberate in African American music and poetry. In it we still hear the chant connecting distant bodies and continents, the relationship between body and speech in African work rhythms. And today's percussion-based rap is the banished talking drum beating an ancient meter and rhythm into a new language.

Bibliography

Bachelard, Gaston. *The Poetics of Space*. Maria Jolas, trans. Boston: Beacon, 1969.

Benjamin, Walter. *Illuminations*. Harry Zahn, trans. New York: Schocken, 1969.

Toomer, Jean. *Cane*. New York: Liveright, 1975.

Vicuña, Cecilia. *Unravelling Words and the Weaving of Water*. Eliot Weinberger, trans. Minneapolis: Greywolf, 1991.

MICHAEL MORSE

My Heart Fills Up with Hungry Fear

Using Margaret Walker's "October Journey"

MARGARET WALKER is best known for her stunning poem "For My People." This is a poem driven by the music of spirituals, as well as by a repetition and drive reminiscent of Whitman. It suggests a childhood steeped in the music of sermons and the rich cadences of biblical language; in fact, her father was a minister in the Methodist Episcopal Church in Alabama and Mississippi. Walker's poetry also has palpable political tones and urgencies, and her imagery often juxtaposes stasis and change—one of the more moving lines in "For My People" comes in the last stanza, when the speaker says, "Let a bloody peace be written in the sky." One interesting assignment is to have students write about what they would want to leave or create for the people they love—their families, their relatives, their peers and teachers, their neighbors—trying to imitate the music of the Walker poem.

> For my playmates in the clay and dust and sand of Alabama backyards
>   playing baptizing and preaching and doctor and jail and soldier and
>   school and mama and cooking and playhouse and concert and store
>   and hair and Miss Choomby and company;
>
> For my people blundering and groping and floundering in the dark of
>   churches and schools and clubs and societies, associations and coun-
>   cils and committees and conventions, distressed and disturbed and
>   deceived and devoured by money-hungry glory-craving leeches,
>   preyed on by facile force of state and fad and novelty, by false prophet
>   and holy believer.

While "For My People" may be Walker's most popular poem, another of her poems (and one of my personal favorites) also captures her ability to balance the good and the bad, the sacred and the profane: "October Journey." I originally found the poem in an anthology of African

American poetry called *I Am the Darker Brother*; it is also in Walker's *This Is My Century: New and Collected Poems*. Walker wrote about the poem:

> I wrote "October Journey," a poem that has multiple meanings in my life, in 1943, after a few weeks at Yaddo, where I wrote the ballad "Harriet Tubman." I was actually making the journey south in October, and "October Journey" expresses my emotions at that time. I met my husband in October, and after 37 years of our marriage he died in October.

I first used this poem with a group of seventh graders. In addition to its personal significance for Walker, October is a highly charged season of birth and death, of brilliant colors warning of literal and emotional winter. We were all struck by the poem's simultaneous address of what's beautiful and scary in a season, in a time of year, on a particular trip, and in the world in general. Note how the opening lines suggest a time of escape, a journey out of bondage, a trip to be taken undercover in dangerous circumstances.

October Journey

Traveler take heed for journeys undertaken in the dark of the year.
Go in the bright blaze of Autumn's equinox.
Carry protection against ravages of a sun-robber, a vandal, and a thief.
Cross no bright expanse of water in the full of the moon.
Choose no dangerous summer nights;
no heady tempting hours of spring;
October journeys are safest, brightest, and best.

I want to tell you what hills are like in October
when colors gush down mountainsides
and little streams are freighted with a caravan of leaves.
I want to tell you how they blush and turn in fiery shame and joy,
how their love burns with flames consuming and terrible
until we wake one morning and woods are like a smoldering plain—
a glowing caldron full of jeweled fire:
the emerald earth a dragon's eye
the poplars drenched with yellow light
and dogwoods blazing bloody red.
Traveling southward earth changes from gray rock to green velvet
Earth changes to red clay
with green grass growing brightly
with saffron skies of evening setting dully
with muddy rivers moving sluggishly.

In the early spring when the peach tree blooms
wearing a veil like a lavender haze
and the pear and plum in their bridal hair
gently snow their petals on earth's grassy bosom below
then the soughing breeze is soothing
and the world seems bathed in tenderness,
but in October
blossoms have long since fallen.
A few red apples hang on leafless boughs;
wind whips bushes briskly.
And where a blue stream sings cautiously
a barren land feeds hungrily.

An evil moon bleeds drops of death.
The earth burns brown.
Grass shrivels and dries to a yellowish mass.
Earth wears a dun-colored dress
like an old woman wooing the sun to be her lover,
be her sweetheart and her husband bound in one.
Farmers heap hay in stacks and bind corn in shocks
against the biting breath of frost.

The train wheels hum, "I am going home, I am going home,
I am moving toward the South."
Soon cypress swamps and muskrat marshes
and black fields touched with cotton will appear.
I dream again of my childhood land
of a neighbor's yard with a redbud tree
the smell of pine for turpentine
an Easter dress, a Christmas eve
and winding roads from the top of a hill.
A music sings within my flesh
I feel the pulse within my throat
my heart fills up with hungry fear
while hills and flatlands stark and staring
before my dark eyes sad and haunting
appear and disappear.

Then when I touch this land again
the promise of a sun-lit hour dies.
The greenness of an apple seems
to dry and rot before my eyes.
The sullen winter rains
are tears of grief I cannot shed.
The windless days are static lives.

The clock runs down
timeless and still.
The days and nights turn hours to years
and water in a gutter marks the circle of another world
hating, resentful, and afraid
stagnant, and green, and full of slimy things.

From the gentle imperatives of the first stanza, the poem moves to the music and autumnal color of stanza two, to the rich textures of stanza three, to the starker imagery of stanza four, to the dream in stanza five and the ungrounded world of stanza six. (Have we arrived in the North, or is the entire journey merely imaginary?) The poem is filled with varied perspectives and voices that juxtapose smooth sailing and bumpy turbulence, celebration and worry. In its balance of the good, the bad, the beautiful, and the ugly, Walker's poetry reminds me of Pablo Neruda's. It also qualifies as "impure poetry," the type of poetry Neruda advocated, poetry that is necessary and unbiased in its effort to capture the "confused impurity of the human condition."

Before we wrote, I discussed "October Journey" with my seventh grade students, allowing them to steer the discussion. What did they like? What worked well? What was confusing about the poem? With one recent group, we focused on the music in the poem. We came up with many wonderful examples of alliteration and assonance. The kids were particularly taken with one image in stanza two ("poplars drenched with yellow light / and dogwoods blazing bloody red"). Many of them said they thought the poem was going to be a "happy" poem because of the initial excitement of the journey, and the narrator's instructions on how to prepare. What about the warnings in the poem, such as "take heed," or imperatives to "carry protection" against "a vandal, and a thief"? I asked them. The kids had read this as the usual volley of parental advice they get when they're heading out the door. The discussion went from there to the rich images of the second and third stanzas. Here kids had noticed that the poem shifts gears a number of times, and begins to present a somewhat ominous and even creepy side. In the fourth and fifth stanzas, we agreed, something evil lurks, and an unpleasant presence creeps into the poem. This subsides for a bit when the train and the theme of going home appear, but it returns in the last stanza, when the "promise of a sun-lit hour dies." Then we discussed the last stanza which, quite frankly, simultaneously confuses and in-trigues me—particularly the first line ("Then when I touch this land again"). Does "this land" refer to the North, a bleak landscape in com-parison with a desired "South," or is it the idealized South appearing cold and lifeless with winter encroaching? I lean towards the former in-terpretation, but the important focus here, as it relates to writing, is the tension or conflict between an imagined or remembered place and the place currently occupied. (A related exercise is to have students write about a place that's not where they are at the moment, but one they can dream of—from the past, or a place that reminds them of life at its best. It might be the place where they live that's somehow improved, or a place that they dream about.)

We also talked about trips they take to visit relatives, to go to an appointment, to go on vacation, etc. The kids were quick to point out that every journey has its shares of highlights and low points, of risks and rewards. At this point I sensed that the students were ready to write.

I asked the students each to choose a month to write about. To help them do this, I had them sit quietly as I slowly called out the months of the year in random order, asking the kids to let associations flood their minds. "What associations do you have with the month in which you read this, and what associations do you have with the month that's six months away from right now?" I told the kids to refer to their lists as they begin to construct their own journeys for their chosen months, the lists that come in handy if they get stuck.

Before I let them loose, I gave them a few final tips:

• Try using a couple of lines in which you offer instructions to your readers. Notice, in the first stanza of "October Journey," how the speaker encourages us but also tells us to be wary. (Kids love the chance to play boss and offer instructions to their potential readers.) If you get inspired, keep going with it.

• Try using repetition to help propel the poem.

• Try to refer to a month or season that's "far away" from the month or season of your poem. (Walker, for example, recalls images of early spring in the first and third stanzas, images that set up a starker, con-trasting picture of October.)

• Try to have images in your poem that help a reader to see, taste, smell, hear, and touch the month that you're in.

• Try to recall at least three images from your past, in the same way that the speaker in "October Journey" does towards the end of that poem.

Below are two examples from the poems that my seventh graders wrote. Most didn't emulate the somber ending of Walker's poem, but they did incorporate her coexisting beauty and bitterness:

November Journey

Nothing is like traveling in November.
Especially traveling home.
November is one of a kind.
In November it can be cold, hot, or in the middle.
Nothing is a November Journey.
Every November I travel home.
Nothing is a November Journey.

I can not describe the beauty of traveling home,
The beauty of the south.
The grass so green, the temperature just right.
I drive by remembering all of this.
The smell of fresh plants and farms.
I drive by remembering all of this.
Nothing is a November Journey.

I find myself drifting.
I am remembering the south.
Stealing the girls' Easter hats
and rolling down the hills.
I smell freshly baked bread.
I hear people singing and dancing.
I am in my childhood.

My flesh starts to tingle
and tears run down my face.
Something inside me hurts.
I am filled with hatred.
I have gone too far while remembering.
I must get out of this state of mind.
Get me out!

I pull over to the side of the road.
I get out of the car.

I sit there for a while, remembering.
Remembering me, remembering the south, remembering my people.
The people whom I sometimes forget.
Nothing is a November journey.
Nothing.

    —*Rachel Mieszczanski*

November Journey

I want to tell you how the breeze rustles through the fallen leaves
How it dances and rustles over the foliage that still grips the tree branches.
Gold.

I want to tell you how the world is a sea of colors.
Gold. Red. Brown. Yellow. Purple. Orange. Gold

I want to tell you about the sky, spread above the earth like the skirt
Of a bride's new gown that she proudly spreads out for the world to
    view.
It is a gray-white color.
The kind of gray that is too gray
To be called White.
The kind of White that is too white
To be called Gray.
But the color, whatever its name, is bright
For the bride's dress is new
And this is her first time wearing it.
Gleaming tassels accent the trimming at the hem. Gold.

As I wade through the ocean of fallen leaves
That crunch under my feet, the breeze
Playfully whistles over my shoulder and tags me on the arm.
"You're it!" it calls.
I chase it, but it is too fast,
For it has been practicing to make the track team,
And I cannot catch it.
The breeze has won the game and laughs.
I laugh too, and collapse onto the grass.
A lone leaf flutters slowly to the ground,
Unwilling to leave its friends and family tree.
It catches my eye. Gold.

But take care on our own November journey, for soon
Night will arrive

The unwelcome guest at a party
And suddenly the dancing and laughter cease.
The air is sharp and shrill and I shiver.
The breeze, now a full-fledged wind, no longer
Wants to play tag, and cuffs me on the ear, rebukingly.
The world is dark.
The trees, too, shiver, for they have lost
Their colorful jackets of leaves.
I look for the gold, but it is gone.
And I am cold.

—*Anna O'Donoghue*

Bibliography

Adoff, Arnold, ed. *I Am the Darker Brother.* New York: Simon & Schuster, 1970.

Walker, Margaret. *This Is My Century: New and Collected Poems.* Athens, Ga.: University of Georgia Press, 1989.

ELIZABETH RABY

Teaching Etheridge Knight's "The Idea of Ancestry"

MOST STUDENTS have not heard of Etheridge Knight, so their attention is half-hearted as I begin to tell what I know of his life. Knight was born in Mississippi, served in the Korean War (ancient days, think the students, and their attention dips a little lower), was wounded (they perk up), and spent a long time in a VA hospital where he became addicted to morphine. Released from hospital, he transferred his addiction to heroin, committed armed robbery for money to feed his habit (by now they are listening attentively), and was sent to prison. There he became a poet, and after his release he continued to battle his various addictions, to write poetry, to publish poems, to give readings, and to return to prisons to conduct poetry workshops for the inmates. Knight died of cancer in 1991.

As I speak I am thinking of his many prison poems, but in a single class period there is no time to discuss them, so I press on. As a participant in the New Jersey Writers-in-the-Schools program, I usually visit a school for four days, and each student is expected to write a poem a day. In today's crowded curriculum most teachers struggle to cover all the required topics, so I try to present a writing lesson that a teacher can use in one class period.

Sometimes I read from an article by William Van Wert about being a team-teacher with Knight at Holmesburg Prison:

> Etheridge began his sessions by telling the men he had done time in an Indiana prison, that he understood what they were going through, and that he didn't want any trouble from anyone. . . . With Etheridge, teaching poetry in the prison was a rallying point, but the lesson was life: how to live it while doing time, how to use doing time, how to reflect upon doing time when one got out. . . . Without his ever saying so, his poems were proof that, while bodies can be incarcerated, words cannot.[1]

I bring a tape recording of Knight's reading at the Library of Congress [2] and sufficient copies of his poem, "The Idea of Ancestry," so that everyone may follow along as he reads it. On the tape, Knight introduces the poem by saying that he wrote it after being in solitary confinement for many days. Called only by his number, he needed to remind himself that he was a man with a name and a family, that he lived in a wider context than that of his present circumstances. Then he recites the poem:

The Idea of Ancestry

1.

Taped to the wall of my cell are 47 pictures; 47 black
faces: my father, mother, grandmothers (1 dead), grandfathers (both dead), brothers, sisters, uncles, aunts,
cousins (1st & 2nd), nieces, and nephews. They stare
across the space at me sprawling on my bunk. I know
their dark eyes, they know mine. I know their style,
they know mine. I am all of them, they are all of me;
they are farmers, I am a thief, I am me, they are thee.

I have at one time or another been in love with my mother,
1 grandmother, 2 sisters, 2 aunts (1 went to the asylum),
and 5 cousins. I am now in love with a 7-yr-old niece
(she sends me letters written in large block print, and
her picture is the only one that smiles at me).

I have the same name as 1 grandfather, 3 cousins, 3 nephews,
and 1 uncle. The uncle disappeared when he was 15, just took
off and caught a freight (they say). He's discussed each year
when the family has a reunion, he causes uneasiness in
the clan, he is an empty space. My father's mother, who is 93
and who keeps the Family Bible with everybody's birth dates
(and death dates) in it, always mentions him. There is no
place in her Bible for "whereabouts unknown."

2.

Each Fall the graves of my grandfathers call me, the brown
hills and red gullies of mississippi send out their electric
messages, galvanizing my genes. Last yr / like a salmon quitting
the cold ocean—leaping and bucking up his birthstream / I
hitchhiked my way from L.A. with 16 caps in my pocket and a

43

monkey on my back. and I almost kicked it with the kinfolks.
I walked barefooted in my grandmother's backyard / I smelled the
    old
land and the woods / I sipped cornwhiskey from fruit jars with the
    men /
I flirted with the women / I had a ball till the caps ran out
and my habit came down. That night I looked at my grandmother
and split / my guts were screaming for junk / but I was almost
contented / I had almost caught up with me.
(The next day in Memphis I cracked a croaker's crib for a fix.)

This yr there is a gray stone wall damming my stream, and when
the falling leaves stir my genes, I pace my cell or flop on my bunk
and stare at 47 black faces across the space. I am all of them,
they are all of me, I am me, they are thee, and I have no sons
to float in the space between.[3]

By the end of the first line Knight has the absolute attention of everyone. His voice has carried the students into that space outside normal time or ordinary distractions—spellbound *is* the proper term for the effect he has had on every class to which I have brought his voice. Knight believed that poetry came to life not on the page, but when spoken. Almost always he recited his poems from memory. Committed to the oral tradition, he wanted his poems to be heard. Consequently I use recordings of Knight reading to introduce his poems to students.

After I turn off the tape and hand out xeroxes of the text, there are usually many questions, primarily about form. "But this doesn't look like a poem. Why the slashes? Why the abbreviations?" I don't have the answers but we discuss possibilities. I mention pauses. I might mention Denise Levertov's idea of the lines of a poem as a sort of score, like a musical score. "Was Etheridge Knight black?" Yes. "What does 'monkey on my back' mean?" (I was surprised to discover that is *already* an archaic term for a drug habit.) "What's a 'croaker's crib?'" A doctor's office, I think. Most students begin to like the form. They imagine potentialities for themselves. They think perhaps they could write a poem, if they were allowed to write a poem like that. "Can we try slash marks?" Sure. "Can we abbreviate words?" Why not?

Next I suggest that the students imagine themselves confined in a prison cell, which is all too easy for some of the students. Whose faces would they choose to pin up on their wall? Why? Who are their ancestors?

Are there snapshots they could imagine, full of the details of a face or a place or a moment in time?

New Jersey has a rich mix of students of every ethnic background. In my experience, all students respond to this exercise, regardless of heritage. They find it interesting to consider where they fit in the long procession of their families and to consider their emotional connection to those who have gone before.

The poem below was written by a young man, a high school senior, who was homeless at the time I visited his class. His mother had a long history of substance abuse.

> My great-grandma was once my
> mom. She taught me not to steal, but
> earn and save. She taught me that
> no matter what your mother does
> she will always be your mother. And
> always treat her like your mother. My
> great-grandmother told me when she
> is gone you will see who is your
> real family is. She knew she was the
> backbone of my family. What I
> mean is she held my family together.
>
> But the day she was gone from
> that day on I knew what
> she was teaching. Everything she
> said was true. Now my family is split
> apart, and everyone's on their own.
> But when she died, it seemed
> like everyone died. When she was
> here, I never got a failing grade,
> I never did the things I do
> now. My great-grandma took
> care of me, my mom and my brother
> and when she died my mom gave
> up on herself.

One young woman in the same class decided she was not happy about any of her ancestral figures, and so with her poem she became the first of her line, the ancestor of her future children and grandchildren, sharing her imagined life story and instructing them. A student in another class shared her predicament, but not her solution:

Where did I come from?
Who's to say.
Mixed with different cultures.
Makes me what I am today.
Unsure of my roots.
Really don't have a background.
Really don't care.
What am I to find if
I go back into the lives before me?
To find that I'm the result of
a slave raped by the white man. So,
I can proceed from shame. My past is gone.

A young woman in the same school had a different response:

I am a black woman.
When I look in the mirror I see a woman with pride and dignity.
When I walk down the street, I hold my head high,
Because I know that I am more than just a color.
Because I know that I deserve respect.
Because I know that I descend from one of the many black women who
   have cultivated the Earth with their bare hands.
Because I know that I have knowledge.
Yes, knowledge.
Knowledge of who I am, and not what other people want me to be.
Knowledge of my ancestors and the burden that the white man had put
   on them.
Knowledge of what is happening today and what tomorrow will bring.
Oh, I am a black woman.
Living in this stereotypical world.
You see, being a black woman is two strikes in this society.
But put downs are pick-me-ups,
Telling me that I can, not that I can't
Telling me that I do, not that I don't
Telling me that I will, not that I won't
Telling me
That I am a highly intelligent being
Not what other people portray me to be.

   —N. P.

The young man from the same school who wrote the following poem
told me and the class that he had never written a poem before, and that

he hated writing. Caught in Knight's spell, this poem of his past poured out of him:

> To tell of my past is very hard to say
> My past was different in many ways
> Cherokee, that was my peoples' name
> And hunting and killing was their game
> To ride free was what we wanted
> White men came and we were hunted
> Living in a peaceful place
> And nothing that could waste
> To live in their time is what I wish
> Not to eat out of a white man's dish
> I want to hunt and eat my food by hand
> And sleep outside with the luscious land
> My people's ways are very old
> My people come from ways that are long
> But now most Cherokees are gone
> Those who are left have forgot our ways
> And gone towards the white man's grave.
>
> —B. J. S.

After that he brought me additional poems he wrote at home each night of my four-day residency. In class he presented a snaphot in words:

Uncle

His hands are gentle
His face looks innocent
But he likes to fight
And intimidate others

He sits in his basement
With a beer in his hand
Waiting for somebody
To try and make him mad.

He sips his beer &
it taste good
Watching T.V.
While his life goes away.

Everyday he sits with a beer

And everyday death draws near
To this person who thinks he's tough
But I wonder if he is going to act
tough when death has put his hand
on him and his beer.

  —B. J. S.

The next poem is from a high school in an affluent suburb:

Back in Time

Not the poses.
Not the dressed up, smiling
everyone has a hand on a shoulder shots.
Not the school picture.

Only when it pulls you in.
The memory that grabs hold of your consciousness
and takes you back in time, to when all of life
was time with these faces.

The picture of my
sister crying on the kitchen table
because she can't get down.
With her fingers in her mouth, her blanket around her neck,
and her big round cheeks bright red and covered in tears.

The picture of my mother and father hiking up a mountain.
They were young, before the children.
A reminder of the mountains they have climbed for me,
and the time in their lives they have given up to me.

My grandfather the roof of the barn he built in three days.
Last year, by himself. Even if he is 65 I wouldn't mess
with the five feet four inches of pure Sicilian nerve.

He could make a man twice his size cry.
My six foot father is scared of him.

My father's parents sitting at their picnic table with my cousins.
I can hear my grandmother, "Bob, would you pay attention to the baby,"
My Grandfather whines back, "Alright, alright."
Then with a wise smile, he turns, winks at you,
and scoops up my tiny cousin.

My mother's sister, with her Dalmatian.
My uncle lying on his chair, taking in the sun.
My other uncle, head back. laughing, with his arm around my aunt.

And then of course my high school sweetheart
He and I, in our snow suits
racing, down the hill
laughing together,
like always.

A time when I was always with them.
When they were real.
Not just pictures on the wall.
That's where these pieces of color-filled paper take me.
These photographs of faces, bring me
back in time.

    —K. B.

Finally, I've included three poems from another New Jersey high school, this one largely Hispanic. The first two, by the same young man, reveal the pain of displacement and separation:

Looking Out

As I look out and see no freedom
People look in and see illegal
The people, I left behind, my family
and many friends of mine
I wonder will the time pass
or go for a million years
and think to myself will I last
Thoughts unclear and a dream that
has failed to appear
cloudiness in a dome
no communication no phone.
Looking out looking in
I see my future getting dim.

Breeze

The ocean breeze through the clouds
the cooly bird drift down the sky as
cars on the open highway and the

waves crashing against the sand as
though on a mission of fatality, green
palm trees symbols of a new creation
and death of the grieving person in
agony after being filled with holes of
glory, holes of tragedy painful hate
that can only be conquered with the
togetherness of brothers and sisters
a big family falling apart at every corner
and seam and that cannot be put back
together because the line of hate is
much stronger than the good of love.

    —W. E.

The final poem is by a young woman who responded to Knight's "he is an empty space" and "I have no sons / to float in the space between."

Silence

There shouldn't be this stillness in this house
There should be the soft gentle voice
of the man I love
There should be the needing cries
of our child but
There is only silence.

I should be able to embrace our baby
and stop his cries
I should be able to see his face
I should be able to hear his laughter
our face, our laughter but
There is only silence.

I want to curl up and die in the silence
like the little one who died in the little space
before he was born into our world.
I want to hear your words for me once again
But there are no lies in the silence
There is only silence.

There is silence from the man I loved
Even when now he speaks I won't hear
my heart is speechless, my soul mute
will they ever be heard again?

Because now in this soundless world
There is only horrid silence
and nothing more.
Silence!

    —A. M. C.

One note of caution: Many schools have strict rules about the use of "ob-scene" language. Preview the Knight tape to determine which poems are appropriate for your class.

Notes

1. William Van Wert. "Holmesburg," *Painted Bride Quarterly* 32/33 (1988): pp. 52–53.

2. Etheridge Knight. *So My Soul Can Sing,* Watershed Tapes (Order No. C-1212, Poets's Audio Center, 6925 Willow St. NW, #201, Washington DC 20012. Cost: $9.95 plus shipping.)

3. Etheridge Knight. *Poems from Prison* (Detroit: Broadside Press, 1968). Also in *The Essential Etheridge Knight* (Pittsburgh: University of Pittsburgh Press, 1987).

RENÉE-NOELLE FELICE

"Knoxville, Tennessee"

Using Nikki Giovanni's Poem

ONE OF MY FAVORITE "teaching poems" is Nikki Giovanni's "Knoxville, Tennessee":

> I always like summer
> best
> you can eat fresh corn
> from daddy's garden
> and okra
> and greens
> and cabbage
> and lots of
> barbecue
> and buttermilk
> and homemade ice-cream
>
> at the church picnic
> and listen to
> gospel music
> outside
> at the church
> homecoming
> and go to the mountains with
> your grandmother
> and go barefooted
> and be warm
> all the time
> not only when you go to bed
> and sleep

This is one of those rare poems that works with students of all ages (including adults) and of many different ethnic and social backgrounds. I have used this poem in inner-city schools, in schools with racially mixed populations, and in virtually all-white schools, all to great effect.

Because of its simplicity, "Knoxville, Tennessee" requires no introduction or vocabulary preparation, and can be read aloud by students.

I usually begin class by handing out copies of the poem. Sometimes a student will volunteer to read it. If no one does, I'll ask for a volunteer or read it myself. We then talk about what they think of it. Occasionally, African American students ask if the poet is black; when they do, I ask what *they* think. Invariably they think she is; I then ask what images in the poem led them to that conclusion. Their responses usually include the foods, the church, and spending time with your grandmother.

Usually the comments are positive, although one high school student was adamant in her assertion that all of the "ands" in the poem made it "dumb."

Often, after I introduce a model poem to elementary school children, I invite them to write a group poem before they write their own individual poems. I have never felt the need to do that with this particular lesson. One of the beauties of the piece is its power to motivate students to be specific (one of the most difficult tasks facing anyone who tries to help children write poetry).

The first time I tried this assignment, one sixth grade boy turned in the following first draft:

> I always like eating those round, small Pizza Hut pies.
> I like the grease;
> the cooking oil at the bottom of the box.
>
> When you open the box,
> the steam comes out at you, pulling you in.
>
> When you sink your teeth in it,
> you feel like you're in heaven.
>
> —*Alex Alves*

This boy was in a class whose previous poetry lacked specificity and imagination. Unsure as to how to proceed during my first visit, I turned to the Giovanni poem, which I had just discovered, and decided to take a chance with it. To my amazement, most of the students responded in a remarkably specific and enthusiastic way.

> I always like to cook rice and beans
> with corn pops.
>
> And I like to cook meatballs.
> I like how I season the meat;

how my hands turn the meat,
and cut the bread.
I like how I give the food out.
It makes me feel good inside.

　　—*Stefanie Montanez*

Although food seemed to hold great appeal, physical activities ran
a close second:

I always like the way my roller skates rumble on the bumpy sidewalk,
rolling up and down the big, busy street,
breeze blowing in my face.
Little rocks and dust blow
in my face, making me sightless.
Still, I always like the way
my rollers skates rumble on the bumpy sidewalk.

　　—*Mecola Hunte*

I always like riding,
feeling the breeze blowing
past my skin;
my legs exercising while
I relax with nature;
my hair up in the air,
blowing behind me;
going up and down a hill;
smelling the trees.
I feel like I am flying,
wrapped in nothing but silk.

　　—*Tanicea Marsh*

In the following poem, another student discards the "I always like"
beginning, while still maintaining Giovanni's use of the specific:

When I am in the water
I feel relaxed and free
from noise and from people.
When I dive to get a ball—
diving and diving—
I feel like a frog,
jumping from leaf to leaf

　　—*Liz-Ann Cox*

Fourth graders in the same school responded similarly:

I always like chicken fried,
mashed potatoes made from scratch,
with melted butter,
corn,
and some salad on the side.

 —*Jackie Lopez*

Although this is a much "leaner" poem than the ones written by the sixth graders, the specificity indicates that the author really got something from the Giovanni work.

Some time later, during poetry workshops with fifth grade classes at another school, I again turned to the Giovanni poem to help the students with specificity. It definitely seemed to help.

One boy, initially blank, finally wrote:

I Always Like

the way the basketball feels in my hands,
dribbling,
then shooting it into the hoop,
gliding through the air
to slam dunk the ball.

 —*Ricky DeLeon*

Another student in the class was so inspired he wrote four in this genre:

I always like
pizza with a lot of provolone,
chopped pieces of sausage,
some diet cherry soda.

 *

I always like a challenge.
I like winning a basketball game
by a three-pointer or a hard move.

 *

I always like to see leaves blowing in the wind.
The soft whisper of the wind.
The wind.

The wind.
Do you know what the heart of the wind whispers? . . .
The wind.

*

Sun bears down on me.
Eating ice cream,
pizza,
drinking cool glasses of lemonade.
Playing basketball in the heat of night
by lamplight.

—*Terrance Dickson*

Perhaps the most motivated student in this group used this form to express her feelings about education:

I Always Like . . .

School.
When the teacher writes math problems on the board,
I'm eager to raise my hand.
The noise in the classroom.
The children running in the gym.
My future to think about.
Teachers who care,
want me to be somebody when I grow up,
not a nobody on the corner of the street
with nothing to do except be alone
with no education.
If I want to be somebody,
go somewhere,
I have to wake up
and pay attention.

—*Robin Williamson*

The universal appeal of Giovanni's poem is manifest in the following examples by tenth graders from a variety of ethnic backgrounds. The first one was written by an ESL student still struggling with the language:

I like to wear a pair of old blue sweat pants.
They have lots of holes.

But they are very comfortable.
I feel energetic when I put them on.
At night, I hang them over a chair,
as they look tired.
I only wear them at home
because they are so exhausted.

    —Edwige Kouassi

The Mechanic

I like to work on cars,
big or small,
foreign or domestic.
I love the smell of gasoline,
mixed with the smell of smoke.
There is no car I can't fix,
But I quit at six.

    —Louis Buono

I Like to Be

in a park
under a shady tree,
watching ants carry bits of bark,
listening to leaves swaying back and forth.

    —Gordon Forquignon

Fall

A cold breeze
ruffling the leaves.
Enchanted colors.
Grandma's fresh apple pie.
The feeling of winter coming up on us,
when mother bundled you up
and said goodbye.
"Off to school," she'd say.
You looked back and there she was,
watching.

    —LarissaSchiano

I always like summer best.
You can Sk8 all day
at the Sk8 parks,
and Sk8 the street,
and grease bearings,
and change wheels
and do tricks
and no school
and get kicked out of places
    for hitting hand rails
and sneak into closed schools
and win competitions
and be on the home team.

    —*Angel Soto*

I like to take photographs.
I like to develop the pictures and
watch them come clearer in the chemicals.
I like it when your pictures
come out exactly as you
saw them when you took them.

    —*Christine Furnari*

The final poem from this high school was written by a ninth grader who spent most of her time during the residency either talking to friends or reading a book. This was the only assignment to which she responded.

My mama's apple pie
is so sweet your tongue will say, "Wow!"
My mama's apple pie's aroma fills the air.
The apples are soft and juicy.
And when my mama makes her apple pie, she says,
"How you want your crust?
And I say, "Fried hard, Mama."

    —*Serena Gerard*

Bibliography

Giovanni, Nikki. *Black Feelings, Black Talk, Black Judgement.* New York: William Morrow, 1970.

LORENZO THOMAS

Woodshedding with Derek Walcott

THERE ARE PROBABLY several reasons why Derek Walcott won the Nobel Prize for Literature in 1992, but it is clear that he is an indefatigable seeker of the possible poetry that can be found in several common varieties of the English language. Albert Croll Baugh once wrote that the history of a language is the history of the people who speak that language; Derek Walcott's works seem dedicated to the mastery of what the English-speaking peoples have created. He demonstrates, also, that one must confront both the history and the language we have inherited or learned: the King's English and the Calypso singer's are both part of our common tongue. What delights and astonishes Walcott's readers, however, provides a truly challenging model for other writers.

Walcott's poem "Saint Lucia's First Communion" was the focus of an evening's discussion at an adult poetry workshop, sponsored by Houston's Inprint, Inc., which met for two hours every Monday night for three months. Inprint advertised it as a "class," but it was actually an opportunity for collective study. Some of the poets were more advanced than others in terms of having had work published in local or national magazines, but we were all avidly interested in exploring each other's work and ideas.

I have always thought of a poetry workshop as similar to a painter's atelier, a musician's rehearsal room, or an actors' studio—a place where the work of art gets done. Jazz musicians, with characteristic hipster wordplay, call it "going to the woodshed." You can make wrong notes, your colleagues may laugh or pick on you, but you *could* come out sounding like Sonny Rollins! In a workshop setting, poems can be used as models in several ways: as a means of opening a discussion, as a cue to subject matter, as patterns to be copied as closely as possible (for the sheer joy of imitation or the pleasure of learning how something works—whether or not you ever want to do it again for yourself), or as a showcase for specific techniques (from which you can select as few or as many as you want).

We agreed to study some of Walcott's techniques in "Saint Lucia's First Communion" and incorporate one or several of them in a poem that we'd present to the workshop for analysis the following week. Walcott's poem is a particularly useful model because it demonstrates why, to achieve its full effect, poetry must be read out loud:

Saint Lucia's First Communion

At dusk, on the edge of the asphalt's worn-out-ribbon,
in white cotton frock, cotton stockings, a black child stands.
First her, then a small field of her. Ah, it's First Communion!
They hold pink ribboned missals in their hands,

the stiff plaits pinned with their white satin moths.
The caterpillar's accordion, still pumping out the myth
along twigs of cotton from whose parted mouths
the wafer pods in belief without an "if"!

So, all across Saint Lucia thousands of innocents
were arranged on church steps, facing the sun's lens,
erect as candles between squinting parents,
before darkness came on like their blinded saint's.

But if it were possible to pull up on the verge
of the dimming asphalt, before its headlights lance
their eyes, to house each child in my hands,
to lower the window a crack, and delicately urge

the last moth delicately in, I'd let the dark car
enclose their blizzard, and on some black hill,
their pulsing wings undusted, loose them in thousands to stagger
heavenward before it came on: the prejudice, the evil!

Our discussion of this poem also led to comparisons (on several levels) with poems by Anne Sexton, Ai, Robert Lowell, and Rumi; and the idea of "several levels" opened into a discussion of archaeology.

Walcott's poem begins with a common *abab* quatrain:

At dusk, on the edge of the asphalt's worn-out-ribbon,
in white cotton frock, cotton stockings, a black child stands.
First her, then a small field of her. Ah, it's First Communion!
They hold pink ribboned missals in their hands,

Almost immediately, however, the rhyme scheme explodes into a vocalic riot:

> The stiff plaits pinned with their white satin moths.
> The caterpillar's accordion, still pumping out the myth
> along twigs of cotton from whose parted mouths
> the wafer pods in belief without an "if"!
>
> So, all across Saint Lucia thousands of innocents
> were arranged on church steps, facing the sun's lens,
> erect as candles between squinting parents,
> before darkness came on like their blinded saint's.

Although Walcott's poem has twenty lines, it adheres to the proportional structure of a Petrarchan sonnet (i.e., a "problem" presented in the octave and resolved in the sestet), with the second part giving the poet's personal response to the scene depicted earlier:

> But if it were possible to pull up on the verge
> of the dimming asphalt, before its headlights lance
> their eyes, to house each child in my hands,
> to lower the window a crack, and delicately urge
>
> the last moth delicately in, I'd let the dark car
> enclose their blizzard, and on some black hill,
> their pulsing wings undusted, loose them in thousands to stagger
> heavenward before it came on: the prejudice, the evil!

The most noticeable technical element of "Saint Lucia's First Communion" is Walcott's creation of *slant-rhymes* using *consonance* ("myth," "moth") and a subtle music of *assonance* and repetition ("stiff," "pinned," "satin"). This use of sound devices echoes the use of *metonymy* that creates the gentle metamorphosis of hair-ribbons into moths and then girls in white dresses into moths/angels that the poet would safeguard in his car, rather than fussily shooing them out (as most of us have done).

Each of us in the workshop played Walcott's changes differently. Clayton Lee's quatrains experimented with alliteration and internal rhyme. Following Walcott's model (five quatrains and the Petrarchan proportion), Lee's poem "Never Too Late" opens upon "A fated place of faded wonder / Lost in a sunset's closing eyes" and builds toward an image that recalls famous paintings by Edvard Munch and David Alfaro Siqueiros:

I'm not who I am he thinks upon
Returning to this deserted place
Vacant now the in between
New mind, new grace, same face

Bright moon slides by in inky sky
Enter again the wet mouth of a dream
Some memories gone, forever misplaced
But never forget it's never too late to hide inside a scream.

Other members of the workshop were less interested in Walcott's stanza form than in his sound devices and use of imagery that changes in unexpected but logical sets of transformations

Kelly Thomas's "Lugosi, Hollywood 1930" imagined director Tod Browning as a mass-media Svengali. Putting words into the famous actor's mouth, she uses assonance and consonance to create a tension appropriate to her subject:

He lit my eyes from underneath
with a grip's pocket flash.
With a director's practiced craft
he carved them dark,
deep-socketed,
all the while praising
my utter foreignness
my muttered phrases,
all the while hissing yes. . . .

Those lines are from the middle of a much longer poem. By the poem's end, the actor Bela Lugosi—wistfully recalling his long-ago film triumphs—turns into something of a real-life vampire, having

Embraced the cool hail of moist soil
cast aside the heat of Hollywood's streets.
Forgot Browning. Forgot Stoker.
Heard only my father's father singing
with the voice of the wolf,
with the voice of the dragon.

It is particularly interesting that the transformations in this poem are both visual and auditory.

Gail Tirone's "The Slow Nights of Childhood" is a memoir of Brooklyn, but a lovely section of this long poem seems to be a variation of Walcott's metamorphosing images. Tirone's vehicle is spatial, however, and the movement resembles a cinematic reverse zoom:

> The slow nights of childhood
> that felt like forever—
>
> Time suspended like an old family story
> told and retold until it becomes myth
> time suspended like a broken kitchen clock
> still hanging on its yellowed wall
> stopped
> time suspended like a radio that won't turn off
> that won't turn off
>
> Time suspended like an old photograph
> closed in an album
> in a rented storage unit
> in another city
> half a continent away

What any of these poems owes or doesn't owe to Walcott's model is, of course, debatable and—as different as they all turned out to be—probably irrelevant. While "Saint Lucia's First Communion" is an uncompromisingly sophisticated work that frustrates any simple paraphrase, teachers of younger writers may find that Walcott's intricate music will bring a response and lead to useful discussions of what rhymes and homophones can do. Black literature is often read for its message or sociological content to the exclusion of appreciating technical or literary qualities, but our experience with Derek Walcott's poem suggests that both aspects of such a work can be useful—on several levels.

Bibliography

Derek Walcott's "Saint Lucia's First Communion" appeared in Eugene B. Redmond's literary magazine *Drumvoices Revue*, vol. 3, no. 2.

KENT ALEXANDER

Playwriting

An Afrocentric Approach

AFTER MANY YEARS of teaching theater workshops in New York City public schools, I have developed a method for using African American literature to teach theater to students between the ages of eleven and eighteen. Because the literature I use generally draws on the authors' personal experiences, students are easily successful and have a positive experience with it. This work seamlessly integrates African American literature into the student's life without any heavy-handed explanations or excess verbiage.

What makes the work so accessible? Most definitely, it is the "hands-on" element. When this atmosphere is created, students don't feel "preached" to, and feel free to explore. This in turn creates a more focused student and one with a deeper commitment to his or her work. Also, a student can participate at a level that allows him or her to feel comfortable. The only pitfall is that some students will tend to dominate the "stage" and must be encouraged to share the limelight.

Each of the following workshop sessions is designed for a single classroom period. To prepare for each session, arrange or have the students arrange the classroom chairs in a circle, or clear a center area for "acting." The object of moving the chairs into a circle is to have everyone face everyone else. You are building a community in which all are accountable and everyone contributes. Inform students that on the day of theater class, they will need to wear comfortable clothing that they feel relaxed in. They might have to sit on the floor, so white slacks or very short skirts are not a great idea. Also, when you're discussing a story, poem or scene, it is important that each student have his or her own copy of the text.

▶   ▶   ▶

The day before the first playwriting class, assign an African American folk tale available in many collections (see bibliography). One book I often use is Julius Lester's *Black Folk Tales*. The book is well-crafted, humorous, and filled with many tales that seem to appeal to teenagers.

Class # 1: Getting to Know Your Text

On the first day, have students sit in the circle and take turns reading the selected story. When we've finished, I ask, "Who remembers one thing that happened in the story?" After students have identified most, if not all, of the memorable details of the story, we turn to what happens in the story and what students like and dislike about it. Ask the students to be specific, citing exact references to make their points. Be sure that everyone grasps the basic elements of the story: protagonist, antagonist, the conflict, and resolution. At the end of this discussion, ask the students if the story reminded them of anything in their own lives.

Next, discuss the characters in the story. Include in this discussion the non-traditional roles that might appear such as a frog, rock, tree, or wind. Inform your students that an actor (male or female) can give these otherwise inanimate elements a voice and character, thereby transforming the story into something new and exciting. Take suggestions from the group about possible roles and how each character might talk. This approach makes the most out of group dynamics and will involve many whose attention might otherwise wander.

Once the roles are clear, pick or solicit from the class a director who will then assign parts (or ask for volunteers).

Class # 2: Improvisation

The purpose of this session is to explore the text in a new light and to give students a chance to play with the story, to learn more about it. Once in the circle, have a student retell the story as it appears in the text. Then discuss other ways the story could be told. Remind the class that the goal of the improvisation is to tell the story in a way that conveys the *intent* of the original. Let the class judge if the actor kept to the story line and what he or she added to the story to make it funnier, clearer, or more contemporary (to name a few choices). This participation will sharpen students' attention to detail. I find that after this initial improvisation, most groups are eager to continue.

Class # 3: Constructing the Play

Inform the students that before they can write a play from their folk tale, they must first learn playwriting format. I like to mention that there are many ways to set up a play, but the following is one that seems to work for everybody.

Write the following on the board for all to see and copy:

Title of Play

Time:
Place:
First action:
Name of first speaking character:
Name of character who responds:

You could then give an example of dialogue, such as:

ROCK: Hi, I'm Rock and this is my land. Get lost!
LIZARD: I'm lizard and I'm staying put till that snake goes away!

The dialogue continues until the entire story is told. Please note that a colon is used to separate the character from the dialogue. In a play, whenever a character moves or does something physical that can be seen by the audience, this is called an "action." When a playwright wants a character to perform an action (laugh, hit, cry, run, etc.), he or she creates a stage direction, using parentheses to indicate it. For example:

ROCK: (*Laughing*) I didn't know that lizards were afraid of snakes
LIZARD: Shhh! (*Lizard peeks quickly around Rock*) He's still out there!

Next, write down (or have a student write down) each action that takes place in the folk tale. These should be in chronological order and will be what your students will use to create the scenes in their plays. A scene is a unit of action that takes place at a single place and/or time.

Here is an example of a play that follows this format, written by a Brooklyn intermediate school student:

The Monkey's Mistake

Time: 9:15 A.M.
Place: On a warm bank of the Tigris River
First Action: Monkey is tossing stones into the river and frowning.

MONKEY: This water sure looks deep.

CROC: Yeas, it is very deep and very wide, Mr. Monkey.

MONKEY: I sure don't want to drown in this old river, Mr. Croc. (*Kicks stone into pond.*)

CROC: Well, you don't have to. I could give you a ride on my back across to the other side. (*He smiles and shows two long rows of crooked, sharp, white teeth*)

MONKEY (*Jumping up and down wildly*): Ha! That's a good one. You ride me across the river?

As you see, the play follows the story line of the popular folk tale, "The Monkey and the Crocodile."

At this point, introduce the concept of monologue, which is used in theater as a way for a character to share his or her inner feelings with another character or with the audience. These feelings may or may not conflict with that character's actions. The monologue can also be used as a device for foreshadowing, or for illuminating the reasons behind an action.

In *Monkey's Mistake*, the following monologue by Croc occurs after Monkey jumps up and down:

CROC (*To audience*): I think this stupid monkey is actually going to take a ride on my back. Wow! Can you believe it? Free schools and silly monkeys. Well, if he rides, I'll dine on fresh monkey tonight! I'll cook him up and have some French fries and gravy. Maybe have a 40-ouncer to go with it. Yeah, it'll be a phat supper and all because of this silly monkey. Mmmmmmm, mmmmm. Tasty!

Have students practice creating examples of dialogue, stage directions, and monologue, so that they can become more familiar with playwriting format.

Class # 4: New Ideas

It is important for all students to know that this is new material and takes some getting used to. Therefore, be certain everyone understands everything discussed so far.

Once you feel that everyone is knowledgeable enough to continue, ask students where they think folk tales come from and how they are passed down from generation to generation. After this, ask for ideas from which to create new folk tales. Examples I have heard in class include *How Ricky Roach Became a Hero, Michael Dunks from Half Court*, and, one of my favorites, *Denise the Dog Wins Her Freedom*. List the students' ideas on the board.

Once you have a collection of ideas, have the students break up into small groups and ask each group to flesh out one of the folk tale ideas in narrative prose. Each group should decide for itself how each story goes and what each element (characters, conflict, and resolution) will be. If the group cannot decide, then step in and decide for them.

Class #5: New Plays

For this session, I ask each of the small groups to choose a representative to read their story to the rest of the class, who then discuss whether or not the story has a beginning, middle, and end. We all decide if the story has a protagonist, an antagonist, a conflict, and a believable resolution. Have the students in each respective group provide any missing components. This empowers students and helps them understand the concept of the group's working together towards the same goal. Always allow time after this for rewriting the story and to insure that the piece is legible.

Then have each group transpose its story into a play, using the format learned previously. Have the groups pay special attention to how their plays begin. Ideally, the plays should begin slowly and build into a conflict. If they start with a full blown argument or a fight, make sure that the play eases off that action and proceeds logically towards the next conflict which, of course, must be resolved.

When the students finish their plays, have each group read theirs aloud to the entire class. Again, everyone should discuss each component of the piece and understand what the conflict is and how it is resolved. If the conflict or the resolution is not clear, have the authors clarify them, or, if necessary, ask the rest of the class to help.

Class # 6: Using Fiction

Using any or all of the following books—*Gorilla, My Love* (Toni Cade Bambara), *Snakes* (Al Young), *Native Son* (Richard Wright), *Invisible*

Man (Ralph Ellison) and *The Collected Stories of Chester Himes*—ask the student groups to choose a small section from the novel or short story to create a short play from. (Note: Please go over each chosen piece yourself beforehand. This way you will be *positive* that the contents of the piece are within your school's standards.)

The chosen section should have a clear conflict and a clear resolution to the immediate problem. One such example is the "rat story" in Richard Wright's *Native Son,* in which the central character, Bigger Thomas, confronts a rat one morning in the family's bleak apartment:

> The rat squeaked and turned and ran in a narrow circle, looking for a place to hide . . . searching for the hole. Bigger advanced a step and the rat emitted a long thin song of defiance, its black beady eyes glittering, its tiny forefeet pawing the air restlessly. Bigger swung the skillet; it skidded over the floor, missing the rat, and clattered to a stop against the wall.
>
> The rat leaped. Bigger sprang to one side. The rat stopped under a chair and let out a furious screak.
>
> "Gimme that skillet, Buddy," Bigger asked quietly, not taking his eyes off the rat.
>
> Bigger lifted it high in the air. The rat scuttled across the floor and stopped again at the box and searched quickly for the hole; then it reared once more and bared long yellow fangs, piping shrilly, belly quivering.
>
> Bigger aimed and let the skillet fly with a heavy grunt. There was a shattering of wood as the box caved in. The woman screamed and hid her face in her hands. Bigger tiptoed forward and peered. "I got 'im, by God. I got 'im."

Class # 7: More New Plays!

Now have each student group transpose the mini-story into a play. This play will have characters from the original story, but can also have additional characters. For example, the rat in the above Richard Wright story *might* have a voice. Also, the younger brother might talk more than he does in the book. When I discuss this possibility, I often compare it to the movies in which new characters are routinely created to further a story line. A great example of this is the film version of *A Rage in Harlem*, adapted from Chester Himes's novel of the same name. The character Danny Glover plays in the film, as well as the dog, weren't even mentioned in the book! In the end, I always encourage freedom as long as it serves the piece. As well as creating the play, the group should also be able to discuss:

1. Why they selected that particular piece.
2. What they think the strength of the piece is.
3. How true the piece is in its relationship to their own lives.
4. What the piece says to them.
5. How to stage it using a large budget and then a small one.

Class # 8: Presenting

At this point, you're ready for some real fun. Have each group present its own play to the class. Each play should, if possible, be casted from within the class. One person from each small group can serve as the director.

Once casted, the play can be performed or given a staged reading. If neither is possible, I strongly recommend that the plays be published in an anthology and that each student who contributes to a play gets a copy. Student writers deserve a tangible reward for their effort, and there is nothing quite like hearing the applause of classmates or seeing your name in print for something you've done well.

Class # 9: Plays from Other Sources

You are now ready for the next step: to develop new plays from other sources. I like to adapt African American poetry and music. I often use the poetry of Maya Angelou, Langston Hughes, and Nikki Giovanni, because these writers use succinct images. For musical sources, I go to Curtis Mayfield, Billy Strayhorn, and just about any blues song. You can also ask the class to choose a current song.

Again, as with literature, *always* screen the lyrics yourself before you agree to permit a certain song to be used. Anything that could be construed as offensive or inflammatory could get you in hot water. I usually explain to a student who protests that these are the school rules and that, outside of school, he or she can write whatever he or she wishes.

The following excerpt from "The Slave Auction" by poet Francis Ellen Watkins Harper is an example that lends itself well to dramatization:

The sale began—young girls were there,
Defenceless in their wretchedness,
Whose stifled sobs of deep despair
Revealed their anguish and distress.

And mothers stood with streaming eyes,
And saw their dearest children sold;
Unheeded rose their bitter cries,
While tyrants bartered them for gold.

At this point, before starting on the actual writing of the play, the student writers need to create a biography for each of the two main characters. These "bios" are what will help to make the character talk and behave differently. I ask for two bios because it is important that the main characters have distinct personalities. Also, when creating conflict in a play, it is crucial to understand what each character wants or does not want, in order to further the action of the piece. In my workshops, I use the following bio format:

Name:
Age:
Family:
Neighborhood:
Wish:
Fear:
Favorite place to be:
Job:
Favorite person (in family):
Favorite person (outside of family):
Favorite thing to say:

Once the bios are completed, I have students read them aloud.

I also like to assign other character developers: an Outside Description and an Interior Life. The Outside Description is what the character looks like to the world. If this character were to get lost, what description can you give that would help someone else find him or her? The *Interior Life* is just that—what the character spends his or her time *thinking* about. Is it video games, money, computers, being safe, new clothes, the Oprah Winfrey Show, or a job? For each of these assignments, decide beforehand how long you want the descriptions to be. I usually ask for more than five sentences.

Then tell the students to start writing their plays as they have done in the past classes. Some students may benefit from writing out their play in a narrative form first. Others may jump right into dialogue. Individual styles will dictate. Do, however, remind the class to make use of all elements of the play (such as the monologue). I also like to have students tell what inspired them before each presents his or her play. Again, when completed, it is a fabulous opportunity for commentary from the class.

Class #10: The Final Project

Finally, it is time for the final project. These plays should be generated in the following way: each group gets together and tells stories that have been passed down from mothers, fathers, grandparents, aunts, uncles, etc. For example, in a Manhattan classroom, a young student named Shaniqua used this family story to create a marvelous play called *The Street of Miracles*:

> My family tells a story about my grandma, my mother's mother, who used to like to take long walks after supper. She said it was to help her food digest, but everyone knew it was really to smoke her one cigarette of the evening. Grandpa was allergic to smoke and she couldn't smoke in the house because of Grandpa. Although it was a small town and very long ago, the family would worry about her out all alone until they heard her footsteps on the porch.
>
> This went on for a long, long time before anything out of the ordinary happened. Then, one chilly evening in October—this was in Indiana where winter comes very early—Grandma went for her walk as usual. She bundled up and started off. Well, as she later told Mommy and everyone else, she was walking where there was an empty lot and she heard the sounds of shuffling papers. Now Grandma was very bold so she stepped into that lot to see what was going on. When she got near the sound, she stopped dead in her tracks.
>
> There was a little baby lying in a bunch of newspapers! She was all black and purple from the cold but wasn't crying or nothing! So, grandma picked up this baby and saw that it was a girl and brought her home. Imagine the look on everybody's faces when she came in this night.
>
> So, they kept the baby, 'cause in those days you could do that, Mommy said. They named her Sojourner after Sojourner Truth because she was a survivor and helped Grandma find her way to loving her.

I like to tell the class that this is how theater was used by our ancestors—to inform friends and family about life and its joys and perils. I go on to say that theater can still be a community event that transforms and educates, bringing people together to celebrate a common history and culture.

No matter what form the story takes, morality tale or joke (I had one student write about his grandfather eating chitlins and biting into a small piece only to force a small piece of corn out of the opposite side and onto the floor, to the amusement of the entire family!), all stories can be put into the "hopper" and analyzed for possible transformation into a play. Again, I permit the group to decide which story they are going to use. I then ask them to create the play using the same tools they developed doing the other plays.

Once the Biographies, the Outside Description, and Interior Life backgrounds are created, the next step is to create a framework in which the main characters are linked together through a conflict which has appeared in an African, Caribbean, or African American story or play that they have read either in class or outside. In other words, family characters are transposed into a dramatic framework from literature.

When Shaniqua rewrote her play, she incorporated the theme of the L.A. riots from Anna Deavere Smith's play *Twilight: Los Angeles, 1992* whose contemporary setting is in South Central Los Angeles. The grandmother (the play's protagonist) rescues the baby (now Asian) from a burning store. In doing so, she begins a new cycle of healing.

In her play, Shaniqua also gave the baby a voice, which gave rise to this touching monologue:

> BABY: I'm cold and don't nobody love me. My mom left me here because she don't be wanting no more kids. She said if I was a boy they might make some room for me and I don't think that is right. I want to have a family keep me and love me and give me pretty things like other girls got. And I want to have my own room so I can play music all night long and talk on the phone. But I'll prolly (*sic*) just get cold and die here. Hey! Here comes a woman and she sees me! Help! Help! Help!!!!!

Once the framework is determined, the students can work on the plays which should, when completed, be staged or given a staged reading.

After each play is performed, the authors discuss the play and answer questions from their classmates. These questions should center on:

- What did the writers get out of the play?
- What did the audience get out of the play?
- What was the conflict and how was it resolved?
- How did it make the audience member feel?
- Is there anything that could have been added to make the play clearer?

Then congratulate everyone on a job well done!

Bibliography

Here is a list of books that I used or mentioned in this essay, as well as other books that might be helpful in developing your own playwriting class.

Bambara, Toni Cade. *Gorilla, My Love*. New York: Random House, 1972.

Busby, Margaret, ed. *Daughters of Africa*. New York: Ballantine Books, 1994.

Ellison, Ralph. *Invisible Man*. New York: Signet Books, 1947.

Himes, Chester. *The Collected Stories of Chester Himes*. New York: Thunder's Mouth Press, 1990.

Kelley, William Melvin. *A Different Drummer*. New York: Doubleday, 1962.

Lester, Julius. *Black Folk Tales*. New York: Grove Press, 1969.

Morrison, Toni. *The Bluest Eye*. New York: Washington Square Press, 1970.

Smith, Anna Deavere. *Twilight: Los Angeles, 1992*. New York: Doubleday, 1994.

Wilson, August. *Fences*. New York: Penguin Books, 1986.

Young, Al. *Snakes*. New York: Dell Publishing, 1970.

ILISE BENUN

Misery Is Fun

Using Langston Hughes's *Black Misery*

PERUSING THE STACKS of the local public library one day, I came upon *Black Misery*, the last book Langston Hughes wrote before he died in 1967. In this little gem of a book, Hughes uses perfectly tuned one-liners to shine a spotlight on twenty-seven humiliating moments of childhood. They are universal moments, some racially universal, some humanly universal, many rooted in the 1960s and the Civil Rights Movement.

As writer-in-residence at the Edenwald-Gun Hill Neighborhood Center, a settlement house in the Bronx, I've had the opportunity to use *Black Misery* with almost every age group: elementary school children in the after-school program, adults studying literacy, senior citizens learning computers, and teachers and administrators in a staff development workshop. I've also used the text at other sites, such as with a group of high school kids in a Summer Youth Employment Program in Hoboken, New Jersey.

Despite its official categorization as a children's picture book (with illustrations by the artist Arouni), *Black Misery* is ideal for use with adolescents and adults, who are able to look back and laugh at situations that, at one time, seemed awful.

Preparation

Though *Black Misery* is a picture book, it is not a straightforward book to teach with. Each page consists of a one-sentence caption and an accompanying black and white illustration, almost all of which raise complex issues and can inspire engaging discussions. So you need to decide beforehand what to focus on, maybe even choose in advance which captions to read, and anticipate what questions might come up and how you'll respond to them.

I've learned from experience that it doesn't hurt to brush up on African American history. When my first class of fifth graders came upon *Misery is when the teacher asked you who was the Father of our Country and you said, "Booker T. Washington,"* I asked if the students got the reference, and was surprised when most answered, "No." Suddenly it was up to me to explain, and I couldn't. I knew who the Father of our Country was but, like many of the kids, I confused Booker T. with George Washington Carver. Lack of preparation made for a missed teaching opportunity.

Be aware that some of the captions need some updating; for example, *Misery is when your pals see Harry Belafonte walking down the street and they holler, "Look there's Sidney Poitier."* Despite the fact that these two actors are alive and well, most children today have never heard of them. I substituted: *Misery is when your pals see Denzel Washington on TV and yell, "Look, there's Martin."* They got that, no problem.

Classroom Presentation

Reading of Text and Discussion

My first goal with any class is to get a lively discussion going, which is usually a challenge, but with *Black Misery* it's easy. In fact, using this exercise as an introductory assignment is a good way to get to know a new group of students.

The first question I ask is "Who is Langston Hughes?" Most know his name; some even know him as the Poet Laureate of Black America or the Shakespeare of Harlem, but in my experience, few students— adults and children alike—can say much more. So, to put *Black Misery* in context, some background on Hughes is necessary.

It's not easy to keep this brief because, according to Faith Berry, author of *Langston Hughes: Before and Beyond Harlem*, he was "one of the most prolific and versatile American writers of his generation, who gained an international reputation and sustained it, at great odds, over four decades." Hughes was a poet, translator, essayist, novelist, dramatist, librettist, folklorist, short story writer, journalist, and world traveler. I list all of these words on the board to show the range of possibilities. Sometimes I read aloud a few of his famous poems and a few not-so-famous ones, as well as a selection from Hughes's series of books centered around his archetypal African American, Jesse B. Simple.

Black Misery includes an introduction by Jesse Jackson and an afterword by Professor Robert G. O'Meally, both of which offer concise and interesting biographical material to choose from. O'Meally writes, for example, that "not only did Hughes know the territory of black America, but his work at its best turned on his genius for . . . the perfectly turned line." The lines in *Black Misery* are examples of this genius.

Berry's biography offers much more material, including the story (in Hughes's own words) of how, at the age of fourteen, Hughes was elected Class Poet, despite the fact that he had never written a poem. "Up to that time I had never thought about being a poet and was rather surprised at being elected Class Poet. In fact, I hadn't expected it. But I guess the youngsters in my class felt I had some rhythm to give a poem. The teacher told us a poem had to have rhythm. And so suddenly a boy called out my name, Langston Hughes, and the whole class said, 'Ay,' unanimously—and that's the way I became a poet.'"

This inspiring story provides a smooth segue to the first caption: *Misery is when you heard on the radio that the neighborhood you live in is a slum but you always thought it was home.*

Often, there's an immediate groan; someone's eyes light up. I ask: "What is *misery*?" A hand shoots up, a definition is shouted out, and the discussion begins. *Misery is sadness. Misery is madness.* Most know well what misery is, although some don't know it by that name. "What else?" I ask, because I want to show them that it's not just one thing, that it's different for everyone, but also the same for everyone. They call out words, associations, opinions—*pain, suffering, hurt.* On the board, I make a list of all the things that misery is, which will be available for them to use when they begin writing.

At Hoboken High, the discussion went very deep, very fast; from the definitions, we quickly moved into a debate about whether one controls one's own happiness and whether people are miserable on purpose. (Most agreed that it is within our power to be happy!) That evolved into an exploration of prejudice, stereotypes, and the impulse to categorize people. Questions flew around the room: "Does stereotyping make life easier for the stereotyper?" "Yes, but it also limits you because then you don't see people as individuals." "What does it do to the stereotypee?" We agreed that everyone can be prejudiced, not only about race, but friends, intelligence, language, hobbies—and we agreed that many traits can be used as an excuse to slap on a label and assume you know a person. It was one of those discussions teachers dream of: everyone is engaged, listening, and responding, and the students speaking with passion about issues that are important to them.

The captions in *Black Misery* work because they're true and they teach emotional truths; there's no faking misery. By sensing which captions elicit the loudest groans, I can show students how to find these truths. We continue reading and talking. "Do you get it?" "I get it!" "What do you get?" The students often relate the Hughes captions to their own experience and sometimes, if I'm lucky, some will spontaneously start making up their own captions. One way to encourage them is for me to start making up my own. Here are two that are inevitably appropriate:

> Misery is when the teacher asks you a question and you're thinking about the answer and you're just about to say it when someone else chimes in.

> Misery is when you're finally involved in an interesting discussion and the teacher says, "Okay, now it's time to write."

Lots of groans with that one. But we're close now; they're almost ready to write. They understand misery, they're making it personal, some of them are already making up their own captions. But before I say "Go!" I give them a last little splash of inspiration by reading aloud what some of my other students have written.

Writing

So as not to create a lot of anxiety, I set some parameters. I give the students a manageable amount of time, usually ten to fifteen minutes, and I ask them to write a minimum of five captions, no maximum. Then I sit down and write along with them. It is extremely important to set the example, to "model the behavior," as the academics say. The students usually go right to work and once they get going, most of them don't want to stop. In fact, one boy in Hoboken kept writing all the way to the end of class.

The "Read-Aloud" and More Discussion

In this final part of the *Black Misery* exercise, I have the students read their work aloud, and most are eager to do so. I like to hear all of their captions, more than once if time allows. Some don't comment on their own captions; in these cases I ask which are their favorites. Or I'll ask the others which they liked best, and why. Before we move on to the next reader, I make sure to comment on at least one or two of each student's captions, pointing out why one works especially well or how another might be improved.

The first time out, many students often write very general captions, so this assignment provides the perfect opportunity to teach the importance and power of specifics. Usually the caption the class considers the best, the one that everyone groans at, is the one most laden with specifics. In Hoboken, it was by Latasha Davis:

> Misery is when you're waiting for the bus and it takes too long so you call a cab and as it drives away you see your bus coming.

Some students, however, don't get it on the first try. One fourth grader's experience beautifully illustrates the process of learning to use more detail. First time around, she wrote this:

> Mad is when you are terrified.
> Love is when you feel good with somebody.
> Scared is when you are very afraid.
> Excited is when you are very, very, very happy.
>
> —*Latisha Knowles*

I pointed out to Latisha that Langston Hughes begins all or most of his captions with the words: *Misery is when...* and then he describes a moment in life that we can visualize. I asked her to replace her adjectives with scenes or situations that included as many concrete details as possible. Here is Latisha's revision:

> Misery is when people sing at your birthday and you say "Don't sing" and they keep singing.
> Happiness is when you see someone special to you, like your ex-boyfriend, and you still love him.
> Angry is when your mother blames you for nothing.
> Misery is when your mother kisses you in front of your best friends.
> Misery is when your teacher said you're not so tall, you're so small.

Latisha was much more eager to read her revised captions, and she got lots of groans.

Why *Black Misery* Works

Misery is concise. I hate to say this but it's true: the shorter the text, the easier it is to engage the students. *Black Misery* works because the captions are short, concise and to the point. Both adults and children appreciate this.

Misery is flexible. No matter what you do with *Black Misery*, it works. There's room for teachers and students to improvise. For example, some students make it their own by substituting other words for Misery, such as Joy, Happiness, or even Responsibility. Here's what sixth grader Shaunta McGann came up with:

Anger is when you say you want to kill somebody but really you don't.
Responsibility is when you are asked to watch your baby brother but
 you just want to hang out with some friends.

Her classmate, Ashante Diggs, wrote:

Happiness is when you're having a sleepover and none of your friends
 fight.
Cool is when you're not too hot or you're not too cold, you're just right.
Being a child is when you have no worries, you can play all day and sleep
 all night and you don't have to pay bills.
Being a friend is when you care for someone, but not in that way.

Misery is fun. One of the challenges of teaching in an after-school program is getting the students involved after a long school day. To do that, writing can't feel like work; in a word, it has to be fun. Hughes makes it fun. He helps us to laugh at our misery, to put it in context—and in turn, he shows us we're not alone.

Misery is universal. Because the text deals so openly with racism, this assignment provides a much-needed opportunity to talk about what really happens and the troubles people have, to tell the stories that are not always welcome in regular conversation. There is room for everyone and every experience of pain. It offers a safe haven for all of us to discuss our experiences, not only as victims of racial discrimination, but also as perpetrators, blinded by our own prejudices. That's the beauty of this exercise: the racism is right there, out in the open. Hughes's captions show how we use someone's skin color to decide who and how he or she is, before a word is exchanged. Here are a few of my favorite captions from *Black Misery* that do this:

> Misery is when you start to help an old white lady across the street and she thinks you're trying to snatch her purse.
> Misery is when you first realize so many things bad have black in them, like black cats, black arts, blackball.
> Misery is when you find out Golden Glow Hair Curler won't curl your hair at all.
> Misery is when the taxi cab won't stop for your mother and she says a bad word.
> Misery is when you can see all the other kids in the dark but they claim they can't see you.
> Misery is when you learn that you are not supposed to like watermelon but you do.

Ivan Croft, Program Director at Edenwald, looked at race from the perspective of joy:

> Joy is when blacks were portrayed as coons and monkeys for years, and yet the #1 recognizable face in the world is Michael Jordan's.
> Joy is finally getting to see *Waiting to Exhale* and finding it as awful as you thought (a man's perspective).
> Joy is when people have accused blacks of being inferior and we invented the traffic light, blood plasma, filament in the light bulb, and more.
> Joy is when Hank Aaron beat Babe Ruth's record.
> Joy is when you appreciate opera, and black and white people look at you oddly.

Despite a lively discussion about prejudice, most of the captions written by my students don't focus on racism. Segregation isn't as overt in the 90s as it was when Hughes's book was published, so racism is now just one of many things that contribute to the misery of my students. Many of their captions have to do with the misery of being poor, or of being a child, or of being a poor black child.

What I love most about the work inspired by *Black Misery* is how much is revealed in a single sentence. Here's what is making kids of the 90s miserable:

> Misery is when a mouse is on your face, arm and bed.
> Misery is when a boy don't want to talk because his mother died.
> Misery is why do little boys and girls have to eat from the garbage.
> Misery is when you are in the class and you think of jumping out the window.
> Misery is when you try to help someone but they think you want something in return.

Misery is when the teacher tells you to stop, but the person next to you doesn't have to.

Misery is when you are mad, like yesterday I was misery because I wanted to stay up but I couldn't.

Misery is when they change your baby at birth and you find out twenty years later.

Misery is when you meet the man of your dreams, then you meet his nice husband.

And here's what makes adults in the 90s miserable:

Misery is when you see an old friend high on crack.

Misery is watching a child cry for a parent that is not there.

Misery is when you go to the hospital to see your brother who used to call you funny names and now he can't speak to you at all.

Misery is thinking you're educated, but you still can't do the crossword puzzle.

The material is so rich, so simple, and so important that I could do an entire ten-week residency using this book and no one would get bored. There are many other related activities that can evolve from this exercise. One class gave me a great idea when they started making up captions for the students who were absent that day. Another idea is to have the students update the references in the Hughes text. On an artistic side, an obvious idea is to have the students create their own line drawings or illustrations to go along with the captions. In fact, a group can work backwards; in other words, draw illustrations and then write captions for them. From there, it's a very short step toward making their own version of *Black Misery*.

Bibliography

Hughes, Langston. *Black Misery*. New York: Oxford University Press, 1969.

SUSAN MARIE SWANSON

Journeys to Our Ancestors

After *Africa Dream*

AFRICA DREAM is a visionary picture book in a simple format. The text by Eloise Greenfield is a poem of fewer than 200 words, and Carole Byard's pictures are all in black and white. This is how it begins:

> I went all the way to Africa
> In a dream one night
> I crossed over the ocean
> In a slow, smooth jump
>
> And landed in Africa
> Long-ago Africa

After reading *Africa Dream* aloud, I like to invite students to talk about their favorite parts. This gives us a chance to revisit various segments and to talk together about the text and pictures. Someone is likely to say that their favorite part is where the child narrator visits the marketplace, and someone else might point out the section that reads "With magic eyes / I read strange words / In old books / And understood." There is a beautiful swirling picture of an embrace at the center of the book, to illustrate the welcome that the child receives: "my long-ago granddaddy / With my daddy's face. Stretched out his arms / And welcomed me home." My favorite part is a picture of children holding hands illustrating this segment of text: "I walked with my cousins/ All over Africa / Lifting my long dress / To step across countries."

Here is one eight-year-old child's response to *Africa Dream*:

> Once I kayaked to Ireland.
> When I got there I was hungry.
> I ate a potato. It smelled good.
> I thanked my great-great grand-
> mother and put my arms around
> her. I heard the drums.
> I went outside. I saw my

great-grandmother. She was only
a girl. I played with her. I said
I have to go back home. Then I
kayaked back home.

    —Patrick

Like the text and pictures that inspired it, Patrick's narrative connects the realm of dreams with the world of ordinary sensory experience. Like the journey in *Africa Dream*, Patrick's dream journey to Ireland leads to an encounter between a child and the child's ancestors, and that encounter is suffused with love. If we had Patrick here with us, we might want to ask him some questions—What was it like in the house where you ate the potato? What did you play with your great-grandmother?—but there is plenty to admire in his piece. The potato and the drums are rich emblems for his Irish heritage, and the kayak is an apt metaphor for individual autonomy.

I have used *Africa Dream* in writing activities in grades one to six, but it has much to offer older students as well. Picture books can make good starting places for writers at all levels. The text of a strong picture book often bridges poetry and prose, and the artwork deepens and extends our experience with the text. Because picture books are generally suitable for reading aloud to a group in a single sitting, they can be compelling focal points for reflection and brainstorming. Other picture books by African Americans that I use in my teaching include *Tar Beach*, a narrative about imaginary flight set in New York City, written and illustrated by Faith Ringgold, and *Mufaro's Beautiful Daughters*, an African tale about two adolescent sisters, adapted and illustrated by John Steptoe, with pictures inspired by ancient ruins in Zimbabwe. Like *Africa Dream*, these books are winners of the Coretta Scott King Award, awarded annually to distinguished books for young people by African American writers and artists. They are widely available in school and public libraries, as well as bookstores.

Activities that help students write their own pieces inspired by *Africa Dream* include 1) some discussion of the word "ancestors" and where our various ancestors lived; 2) a review of the five senses and how they can help us write about our own dream journeys; and 3) a look at how *Africa Dream* is full of action and how we can use action in our own writing. Sometimes young writers find it helpful to practice pointing to their eyes, ears, and other parts of the body related to the five senses, to look at material written in ancestral languages, or to explore modes of dream travel through creative movement. Some teachers invite students to draw or paint, as well as write, in response to picture books. A good picture book like *Africa Dream* opens up rich and flexible possibilities for writing and other creative work.

Reading aloud work by other children helps me talk about ancestors, review the five senses, and describe ways of writing with action. I find it helpful to tell anecdotes about other students who have tried this writing idea and to paraphrase writing by others, as well as to read example pieces aloud. This strategy helps me open as many doors as possible, and often students find it exciting to be part of a group of people who have explored an idea in writing.

There is something nourishing about placing ourselves in the world of our ancestors. It is, among other things, a world without television and electric lights. One student, Heidi, wrote about sitting by the fireside on a cold evening in Germany, in a place so quiet that she could hear a child's breathing through the wall. Faced with the question of what to do with a free afternoon in long-ago Guatemala, Julio was momentarily flummoxed, until it struck him that he and his companion could play on the beach and even build a raft together. Ryan knew a lot about farming. Urged to draw on that, he described how he would help plant seeds by hand in long-ago Poland, rather than using the farming machinery familiar to him. When Christine felt that she didn't have enough background knowledge to write from and was about to give up, she was struck by an idea that excited her: she would open gifts from her ancestors! "I ripped off the paper of the first present. It was an old-fashioned doll!" Later in the piece, she plays dolls with her long-ago cousins. When it starts to rain they run inside for hot chocolate: "We all sat by the fire and sang songs. Then I woke up and somehow I knew that it wasn't a dream."

Including sensory details can help us slow down the pace and deepen our writing. Moreover, in these journeys to our ancestors, sensory description can delineate connections between past and present, as eight-year-old Teddy's piece demonstrates:

In my dream I went to Italy. I ate spaghetti. It was very spicy, but it was very good. It tasted just like my dad's spaghetti sauce. It has tomato sauce, peppers, sausage, onions, pepper, and some more stuff in it. The dinner was very good and I just can't wait 'til I have it again.

Writing about her Ojibwa heritage, Teddy's classmate Laura wrote about a walk on the shore of a beautiful lake:

I made a bucket out of birchbark and filled it with water and took a drink. I felt the cool water down my throat.

(It was a hot summer day, and the children had just come from a break at the drinking fountain down the hall.)

Thinking about ancestors also raises questions.

What if my ancestors came from different countries?

I might answer this question by telling about Anna, who wrote two dream journeys, to Scotland and to Sweden. In Scotland she helped rake the hay into piles and played bagpipes; and in Sweden she baked sugar cookies with her cousins, swam in a lake, and picked berries. Often, students just need the simple reassurance that they can make a good choice about where to begin writing. Maybe a visit to one of several possible ancestral countries sounds more fun to the writer. Many young people know more about one part of their ancestry, and they might do well to start by writing about what they know best.

What if I don't know where my ancestors came from?

We can urge the student find out, of course. But this writing idea is flexible enough to accommodate writers who don't know the answer. Mikayla, a second-grader, wrote about a dream journey to her grandmother's present-day house in Wisconsin, ending this way:

We went in the backyard. My grandma said, "See the strawberries. They taste so, so good. Do you want to pick some?" "OK," I said. I ate some and after that I said, "I'm getting homesick, Grandma." She said, "I'll hold you." I said, "O.K."

What if I want to write about a different kind of journey?

We need to say yes to student writers as often as we can. I usually remind them about some basic elements of the writing idea the group is exploring. I ask them to try to bring those basic strategies to their work on their own new idea. Kim, a fourth grader, decided to write about an imaginary visit with a grown brother whom she missed very much. When we talked about using the five senses and describing action, Kim seemed sad about how faint her brother was in her memory. I urged her to think about ways the two of them could have fun. In her piece, she goes sightseeing in Alabama, and then smells the pizza her brother has made:

> I tasted it. It was good. I touched it and I burned my fingers. I heard the dogs barking. We went on a horse ride all around town. The horse was galloping. And then I saw my mom and dad riding a horse. They came by us.

Relationships with long-ago people can be complicated, even painful. Rebecca wrote about a visit to Israel. The child in the story is very careful not to let on that it smells horrible in the hut, not wanting to offend her ancestors; but when they play with a dreidel she wins every single game. Zolly's visit to Russia is rooted in a tragic family story: "My mom's mom was only in third grade when a soldier kicked down the door and took her away, and I woke up!" Lea, a fourth grader, wrote a vivid description of being dragged away from home by an errant star and carried away to a place where an ancestor slaps her hard across the face. When the child slaps the angry aunt back, she magically returns to her own home and beloved parents.

Maya's dream journey to Nigeria begins like this:

> I dreamed I went to Nigeria. Long-ago Nigeria. My body grew as long as the world. My body curved around the world and I did a somersault and landed on my feet in Lagos, Nigeria. I went to the market where I saw my great grandma Ya-potato selling potatoes. She said in a strange language "Potatoes for sale!" I could understand her. I said to her in the same strange language, "I'll buy a dozen potatoes, please."

Maya's understanding of her African heritage emerges in many ways in the long story that she wrote. The heat is oppressive; the work, backbreaking; the roles, clearly defined:

> I saw Ya-potato as she stumbled home from work at the market. "Time to make supper," she said. We went out in the sticky hot sun. My cap stuck to my hair. I wanted to faint in the hot sun. I picked corn as long as I could. I was getting a terrible headache. My long pants stuck to me. I couldn't stand it any longer. "Ya-potato," I said. "Can I go inside?" "No," said Ya-potato. I dreamily watched a couple of boys playing ball. Earlier in the day, I had wished I could play, too. But right now all I wanted to do was get cool.

On her way to the well, the girl faints. She is revived by women who bring buckets of water. Then comes a rumble of thunder, and with suppertime comes the rain. The story concludes:

> As I danced inside the door, I smelled supper. I hurried to serve all the other people first before I could sit down. It was a wonderful supper. I went to one of the mats on the floor. I didn't go to sleep for awhile. I happily listened to the rain on the roof.
> "Maya, Maya, time to wake up!" I stretched out and remembered.

Maya's knowledge of one of her ancestral cultures was extraordinary, and *Africa Dream* gave her a new way to explore and honor her identity. Most children will write dream journeys with less complex detail, but no matter. The chance to do some work, celebrate, and eat a meal with one's ancestors doesn't come along every day, and Eloise Greenfield and Carole Byard have opened the doorway for us.

Bibliography

Greenfield, Eloise. *Africa Dream*. New York: HarperTrophy, 1992.

Ringgold, Faith. *Tar Beach*. New York: Crown, 1991.

Steptoe, John. *Mufaro's Beautiful Daughters*. New York: Lothrop, 1987.

LEN ROBERTS

First Line / Rhythm Poems

Taking Off from Langston Hughes

IN THIS EXERCISE, which works well with students in grades 3–12, I provide a first line of poetry they may use as a rhythmical base for their writing. Although the students may not be (and do not need to be) adept at counting stressed and unstressed syllables, they will be able to *hear* the rhythm, or prosody, of the line—and that rhythm or beat will help them to create more lines.

This rhythmical line also may serve as a refrain; if the students run out of words, I encourage them to repeat the base line and let new words come. The students may create a poem by using one or two rhythmical lines (as in Heather Mateyak's "I Have Seen") or by using several rhythmical lines (as in Sonasha Braxton's "Let the Rain Kiss").

Although rhythm and prosody, which are the very core of poetry, form a complex topic, the teacher may still use them to motivate writing without spending two weeks defining them. Here's what I do.

Start with a Strong, Rhythmical Line

Start with a phrase or sentence that has a strong rhythm; you do not have to count stressed and unstressed syllables, just listen to it.

One of several lines I have used is "Let the rain kiss . . ." from Langston Hughes's wonderful poem, "April Rain Song":

April Rain Song

Let the rain kiss you.
Let the rain beat upon your head with silver liquid drops.
Let the rain sing you a lullaby.

The rain makes still pools on the sidewalk.
The rain making running pools in the gutter.
The rain plays a little sleep-song on our roof at night—

And I love the rain.

▶　　▶　　▶

89

After I read the poem to the class, I put the words "Let the rain kiss" on the board and ask the students what kinds of people, places, or things *their* rain might kiss, stressing that their objects can be imaginary as well as real, and that the objects may be ugly as well as beautiful.

Once the students understand they can have their rain kiss *anything*, they usually become very enthusiastic and call out image after image, which I put on the board with the reminder that they may "borrow" any image that will help their writing. I also try to get them to provide images from their everyday lives, such as the maroon Ford Taurus, the American flag, or the bully on the corner. Usually the combination of such realistic images with their imagined details—such as Caitlin Jacob's "dirt from the toenails of the lonely weeping women" (in her poem below, "The Music")—produces good, interesting poetic associations.

After we have plenty of images on the board, I talk about the transformative power of rain, how it moistens the earth and helps things to grow, asking the students for examples that are real and imagined, stressing that the rain should kiss things other than plants. Then I put a "so" on the second line, just beneath "Let the rain kiss," and I ask the students to create a poem that follows the same structure, such as:

Let the rain kiss the hungry,
so they shall have bread in their mouths.

If, after a few such images, the students get stuck, I encourage them to repeat the line "Let the rain kiss," with the hope that it will fuel their imaginations and help them to continue writing, as the example poems below demonstrate. Then we write.

Tamika Vactor, an eighth grade student, used wonderful transformations in her poem:

Let the Rain Kiss

LET THE RAIN KISS
Teenage mothers with their babies &
Broken beer cans or bottles.

LET THE RAIN KISS
Jesus so He can
Touch Drunk People,

Cigarette butts, Smokers &
Drugs.

LET THE RAIN KISS
12- & 13-year-old girls
So they don't get
Pregnant.

LET THE RAIN KISS
My brother so he
Can get a good
Education.

LET THE RAIN KISS
The Flowers in
Yards,
Lilies & Roses.

LET THE RAIN KISS
My mother so she is
Strong before she dies
Walking
Up three flights of stairs.

LET THE RAIN KISS
My Aunt Avie so she
Can find another job
In Pittsburgh.

LET THE RAIN KISS
Me for when my grandmother dies
I can be strong.

LET THE RAIN KISS
Me so I can go to Medical School.

LET THE RAIN KISS
Bloody Jesus for making people
Believe in themselves.

❧   ❧   ❧

Two of the great benefits of this exercise are that it helps students to break expected associations (through the use of a catalogue or list of images rather than a narrative) and that it provides students with a way to *begin again* once their imaginations flag. The refrain "Let the rain kiss" provides them with a strong, repeating rhythm that helps propel them toward accepting new images or ideas that pop into their heads. This openness to "popping" allows the writers great imaginative freedom.

The intensity of emotion and vivid imagery in the following poem by eighth grader Sonasha Braxton show the power a beginning writer may get from this exercise:

Let the Rain Kiss

Let the rain kiss
the starving children in Bosnia
their hunger is great
Let the rain kiss
the trash cans
in the dark alley
Let the rain kiss
the chairs toppled over
and couches with ripped seams
in front
of my garbage
Let the rain kiss
the small child
abandoned and unwanted
Let the rain kiss
the rooftops
so they bless
the keepers of the house
Let the rain kiss
the ark
in the possession of Noah
Let the rain kiss
the blooming flowers
in the midst of winter
Let the rain kiss
the cross
the barren field
that needs sunlight
Let the rain kiss
the picture of Jesus
hanging on the basement wall
Let the rain kiss
the father
the mother

the son
the daughter
for they have no place to go
Let the rain drown
the racism
the discrimination
the hatred
the prejudice
and let them flow into
the cleansed waters
so they also
can become cleaned
Let the rain kiss
the grass
for it is brown and withered
from drought
Let the rain kiss
the finger puppet
in the decrepit
aging trash can
the puppet no longer
in use
because mother and son
have drifted apart
Let the rain kiss
the old drunk
who staggers up and down
the streets
limping on one leg
the other lost in Vietnam
Let the rain kiss
the six-year-old
in the small apartment
who has nightmares
about where her father
is now
she doesn't quite understand
the meaning of death
Let the rain kiss
the earth
so the flowers
will bloom
life will flourish

anger and hatred will
become happiness
and the world will become
a better place
Let the rain kiss.

➤   ➤   ➤

One variation on this exercise uses the same basic phrase, but asks the students to substitute strong verbs in place of *kiss*, as Kira Botkin, a sixth grade student, does so well in this excerpt from her poem:

Rain

. . . let the rain *grasp*
the widow's piano
so it may play joyously again . . .
let the rain *wash*
the mist away from
a divorceable couple
so they may see eye to eye again . . .
let the rain *probe*
the farmer's fields
so they may never know drought
let the rain *pummel*
the drug dealers
and fling their merchandise from them. . . .

➤   ➤   ➤

Another variation of "Let the rain" is "Let the music," as in these few lines from a poem by Caitlin Jacob, a seventh grade student:

The Music

Let the music swirl the reds and blues of the fallen tree in
   the forgotten painting
Let the music comfort the uneaten wedding cake
Let the music wash the dirt from the toenails of the lonely
   weeping women
Let the music stop the sweet man from making unimaginable
   mistakes.

➤   ➤   ➤

Variation: "Back in the night when I was born"

Any line will work for this exercise, so long as it strikes your ear as having a strong rhythm. One I have used successfully with students in grades 3–9 is "Back in the night when I was born . . .":

Back in the Night

Back in the night when I was born
the moon grew blue
and in the darkness I saw
black shadows of people
standing above me.

Back in the night when I was born
I heard the sounds of voices
talking like the wind pushing
the ocean water.

Back in the night when I was born
I saw the beautiful stars glowing
turquoise and gold,
I heard the clock telling the time
of life.

Back in the night when I was born
I prayed time would be endless
and not be counted like the waves
of the sea floating upon
each other for infinity.

> —*Roberta Setzer, seventh grade*

❧   ❧   ❧

Another line that evokes strong emotions and images from students in grades 7–12 is a slight variation of one from Allen Ginsberg's "Howl": "I saw the best minds of my generation destroyed by madness, starving hysterical naked, . . ." I shorten this to "I have seen the best minds of my generation . . ." and ask the students what they think is happening to *their* generation. The responses are startlingly powerful. This poem is by Heather Mateyak, a ninth grade student:

I Have Seen

I have seen the best
minds of my generation

wasted on alcohol and
high on drugs.
I see them on Mauck Chunk Street
and by the Comfort Station.
I see them as they drive to school
and on Piercinni's corner.
I have heard the best
minds of my generation
yelling obscenities
and starting fights.
I hear their lighters
and their beer can tabs.
I see their graffiti
and outened cigarettes.
I hear their deafening music
and old Novas.
I see young mothers with bent heads
and unfeeling fathers telling jokes to buddies.
I hear their babies whimper
and their baby carriages squeak.
I feel their worthlessness,
I feel their loss of dreams.

                              ▶   ▶   ▶

Another variation is to have the repeating line *end* each stanza, as in this poem by ninth grader Daltha Freeman:

Untitled

    I—Trojan Man

I've seen the best minds of my generation
Get drunk in the basement at a party
Get high in the bathtub
Get screwed in the closet
Get pregnant 'cause of a dare
Get killed by a gunshot
Get buried by their best friends
It sucks to be cool

    II—Newport

Bang, Bang
You're dead
You're high

You're drunk
You're hard
You're nothing
It sucks to be cool

III—Jack Daniels

Out of 1500
In a school
20% don't smoke
10% don't screw
5% don't get high
3% don't get drunk
1% don't do anything
But lie in a grave
It sucks to be cool

IV—These are my only friends

All I have to say
To these fools on the street corner
Is
It sucks to be cool
It sucks to be you

>   >   >

Obviously, the repeating line can be from a favorite poem, song, adage, proverb, or slogan, as long as it sets up a dominant rhythm and provides the students with a baseline that will propel more words. Of course, the content of the line, as well as the pre-writing discussion, will greatly determine what kind of material will appear in the poems.

Also, the length of the first line will determine the line lengths throughout the poem: short beginning lines will tend to create short-lined poems, and so on. Additionally, if the first line locates the students in a specific, image-laden place, the resulting poems will tend to be imagistic; if, on the other hand, you begin with a more general idea, such as "I have seen the best minds of my generation," try, in pre-writing, to steer the students toward specific images.

Many good, strongly rhythmical lines may be found in Langston Hughes's other poems. Following is a list of some I have found useful in helping students to write poems.

"Did you ever go down to the river? . . ."
(from "Reverie on the Harlem River")

"In time of silver rain / the earth . . ."
(from "In Time of Silver Rain")

"When Susanna Jones wears red . . ."
(from "When Sue Wears Red")

"She stands / In the quiet darkness . . ."
(from "Troubled Woman")

"In times of stormy weather . . ."
(from "Strange Heart")

"When I get to be a composer . . ."
(from "Daybreak in Alabama")

"I pick up my life . . ."
(from "One-Way Ticket")

"Well, son, I'll tell you: / Life for me ain't been no crystal stair . . ."
(from "Mother to Son")

"The rent man knocked. / He said, Howdy-do?"
(from "Madam and the Rent Man")

"I play it cool . . ."
(from "Motto")

"Don't let your dog curb you! / Curb your doggie / Like you ought to do . . ."
(from "Warning: Augmented")

"God knows / we have our troubles, too— . . ."
(from "High to Low")

Bibliography

Hughes, Langston. *Collected Poems.* New York: Alfred A. Knopf, 1994.

JANICE LOWE

The Delicate Rumble of Pianos

Using the Work of Bob Kaufman

I HAVE INTRODUCED children to the poetry of Bob Kaufman in all of my poetry residencies. There is something about Kaufman's love of jazz and blues that communicates profoundly with children raised on compact discs, music videos, and Walkmans. In the 1970s, in addition to participating in organized music activities, my friends and I sang and danced on the way to and from our de facto segregated elementary school in a working/middle-class African American neighborhood in Cleveland. We boogied and sang to 45s during breaks and listened to as much radio at home as we could get away with. I remember going to sleep with earphones on and waking up tired, but happy to have heard my favorite songs too many times a day. From hand games and jumprope rhymes to Earth, Wind & Fire and Led Zeppelin, we lived our lives in music.

Many of the kids I meet in New York City public schools have a similar devotion to music, but fewer chances during the school day to express that love. Since arts programs in the schools have been cut back in recent years, children are less likely to be choir, orchestra, or band members than my classmates and I were. But my students and I re-claim African American, Afro-Caribbean, and Latin dance terms and give the words new (and sometimes fantastical) meanings. We write variations on the songs of our favorite recording artists and make funny stories whose characters include Biggie Smalls, Q Tip, or Snoop Doggie Dog, the colorful names of contemporary rap artists. After a couple of sessions, the children's poems start to take on some charac-teristics of their favorite music and dances.

Bob Kaufman was interested in documenting the music that he loved. Of course, I could say the same thing about his interest in visual artists, philosophers, and poets—he was anything but one-dimensional. Because of the expansiveness of his interests, his jazz poems were not of the let-me-throw-in-a-few-scat-syllables school. He infused his writing with biographies of musicians and composers, with the dilemma of being innovators in a time when Blacks were considered inferior, and with the tremendous high that comes from music-making, the extension of that rush through drug use (and the resulting deterioration) with an ancient way of art-making that expresses the everyday and the extraordinary in abstractions akin to the surreal shapes of African culture. Kaufman's words blow onto the page as theme, variation and transformation, the versatility that makes every jazz player a composer and jazz a unique form of music. In Kaufman's work, one feels propelled into other realms by emotion/energy/sound. His jazz-injected words become musical notes of varying levels of intensity.

Poet Julie Patton has developed a free-association exercise in which she reads an evocative text aloud while students write, allowing themselves, if they wish, to be influenced by the reading. In using the same method with seventh and eighth grade students at I.S. 59 in Queens, N.Y., I asked students to write down words and phrases inspired by my reading of Kaufman's poems. But first I had them read his poem "Walking Parker Home." Then I asked one student to read the poem very slowly to me while I wrote associatively on the chalkboard. Kaufman's first two lines are:

> Sweet beats of jazz impaled on slivers of wind
> Kansas Black Morning / First Horn Eyes

I can't recall what I wrote, but it might well have been something like this:

> sugar reggae rhythms q-tip my windy waiting ears calling the early
> light to my Cleveland attic eyeball room

I took up a whole section of the chalkboard with this craziness, which the students found funny or just plain odd. However, they got the point. (Older students seem to need more explanation.) Then, to the sound of my voice slowly reading Kaufman, the students took off on their own associative flights:

> Dark night, a jazz man playing the saxophone
> making loud notes which cats can hear in the alley in the

back of the club, crying so that everybody can feel his pain.
Then burns a piano player and a woman singer. But
yet they sound sad too. Giving people sadness even
in its faraway galaxies. It is raining.
The spotlight looks like a moon on his head,
the songs of his bad love. Everybody feels his
pain and is hurting. The cold breeze sweeps
the audience. They try to leave but can't because
they love the sadness. They all have learned about
the other side. They all want to see the sun
again but don't want to leave the darkness.

  —Brendon Davis, eighth grade

Swinging visions
of the soul
Collapsing into thin air
The terror of being
left alone
Whirls around like
a gusty wind circling
like seagulls
over a body of water
The legacy of being
forgotten, but feeling
the burning rage
  of the soul

  —Samantha Hope, eighth grade

Worried Bee-bop
alternating City God
beating spirituals on dead kings
Organized crime dog
Travels of outer body
highs
Looking down on
death & hate. Scatting
no hope of beauty, tumbling
off peak. Wings. Rebellion of
rich birds dying quickly
from uncured pain.
Evil above. Disappearing

music in fog. No return
shrinking of no accomplishment
by enraged humans.

    —*Joslyn McPherson, eighth grade*

Candles melting over a crystal ball
Pit decapitations & mystic walls
Golden weapons, unlearned lessons, lyrical Armageddon
and freestyle sessions
money collecting, baby expecting
Composition, officer corrections
Swinging doors, singing chores, king and more flinging forth
Head bangin', red wagons, tails wagging
Bloody nose, cruddy clothes, fuddy duddy foes, & muddy Girbauds
Uncertain existence, indefinite distance, hesitant resistance
Unwanted assistance
Loud cries, proud guys
Now's the time

    —*Brandon Grey, eighth grade*

While Brandon's poem is a fast stream-of-consciousness rap, both
jazzy and clever, Samantha and Joslyn's pieces examine the theme of
alienated musicians playing not only for survival but to be appreciated
and remembered. Some of Joslyn's phrases ("tumbling off peak" and
"scatting no hope of beauty") suggest the quirkiness and speedy playing
of bebop, the style of jazz that Charley (Bird) Parker helped to originate,
as well as the twist and turns of fate. Brendon's beautiful narrative explores the side of human nature that enjoys melancholy.

Once a teacher encourages students to draw upon their consider-
able capacity for empathy, the resulting writing can be cavernous in its
depth, sometimes surprisingly mature. Like small children noticing
flowers and birds for the first time, middle school students are amaz-
ingly sensitive to and empathetic towards life's tragedies and contradictions. Because these students are often underestimated, they have a
keen sense of the fair and unfair. All those emotions, coupled with their
ricochet energy, can generate wonderful poetry, and with this free association exercise, they can project themselves and their emotions on
the page.

"Walking Parker Home" is a poem in movements. In those movements, the reader learns about Parker's life: we come to know him as a boy; as a young sax player influenced by elder musicians Coleman Hawkins and Lester Young; as an intellectual trying to find the time to create; as a resident of New York City; as a drug addict; as a corpse; after his death, as an icon, a spiritual and cultural force. This is weighty stuff for seventh and eighth graders to digest. The biography in the poem is delivered in the abstract. Words fly by too fast for comfort, but it is the difficult life lived, which we discuss at length, that piques their interest.

♪   ♪   ♪

In a fourth grade classroom at P.S. 75 in the Bronx, my students were equally fascinated by Kaufman's life. They were especially fascinated that he had traveled around the world as a merchant marine. The photo of him on the cover of his book *The Ancient Rain*, however, jolted them a bit. Before seeing the photo, Kaufman, to them, was a romantic figure with the freedom to travel and see things. Although he is dressed nattily in the photo—in a Superfly-wide brim hat and a beautiful poncho over a white tunic-like shirt, with a handlebar mustache and handsome features (his profile in the mirror behind looking younger than the head-on stare into your soul)—the kids in this mostly Nuyorican community said, "He looks ugly," "He looks old," "He looks like a bum." I spoke with them about Kaufman's drug addiction, his stay in a mental institution, and the difficulties of being Black in America. "But he looks Spanish," the students said. So we talked about the range of skin colors, hair, and features in our own families, about how blackness is more than race. The students were more concerned with his world-weariness. They recovered from the shock of the photo and immersed themselves in the legacy of a great poet. Jessica Gonzalez, impressed with Kaufman's traveling but also concerned by his death, wrote:

Dear Bob

> How can you do
> all these things
> How did you die?
> This is what the Blues means
> to me. The sky, the river

and oceans, when you fly
into the sky.

That's
what the Blues means to me.
I wish I could go around
the world eleven times.

In the same free-association exercise I described above, one student responded to "Blues Notes," Kaufman's ode to Ray Charles. Kaufman's poem reads:

Ray Charles is the black wind of Kilimanjaro
Screaming up and down blues,
Moaning happy on all the elevaors of my time

Smiling into the camera, with an African symphony
Hidden in his throat, and (*I Got a Woman*) wails, too.

He burst from Bessie's crushed black skull
One cold night outside of Nashville, shouting,
And grows bluer from memory, glowing bluer, still.

At certain times you can see the moon
Blanced on his head.

From his mouth he hurls chunks of raw soul.
He separated the sea of polluted sounds
And led the blues into the Promised Land.

Ray Charles is a dangerous man ('way cross town),
And I love him.

for Ray Charles's birthday
N.Y.C. / 1961

The student, Yaziri Perez, responded:

I love the Blues notes. The mountains
are big, bigger than me. The songs
are beautiful and I wail to me. I stand up
and start to wail. I said it in the sky
and I started to wail to my dad. I went
to another sea. The sky was beautiful.
He left me alone by my side. He left me.
He is a bad guy God punished. That is
for me. Please do it for me.

In Yaziri's poem, the cosmic accident, the wind and water involved in the birth of a woman refer to an accident involving singer Bessie Smith described in Kaufman's poem. Yaziri becomes empowered with song. The subject of Ray Charles and music empower Yaziri to sing her own blues.

Another reason I love reading Kaufman with young people is his sense of play. On the page, he reveled in exploring the child within himself: he was constantly creating new languages and worlds, wacky political stances, and irreverent philosophies. Words become keys to dimensions other than our own. His "Abomunist Manifesto," a poetic takeoff inspired by the "Communist Manifesto" and McCarthy-era paranoia, pokes fun at the both left-wing and right-wing politics. Unafraid of society and its many labels, Kaufman wrote a comic manifesto that celebrates individuality, proclaiming an allegiance only to oatmeal cookies!

After reading aloud excerpts from the "Manifesto," including parts with nonsense language that the kids found amusing, I asked seventh graders to draw up their own manifestos, both serious and tongue-in-cheek:

> dogs are lousy cats
> an alcoholic can't make it with one swig
> skinny people need to eat less food
> hey look at that dead bird falling
> the clouds are big ice-cream cone scoops
> just waiting to be licked
> when you read you're lousy
> when you don't read you're even lousier
>
> —*Brandon L. Galloway*

> Soda bottles explode while open
> Glass falls on the floor but doesn't break
> People watch TV when it's not on
> Friends eat ice cream without the cream
> Love is an Easter pink that drops on occasions
> Angry smells like burnt toast
>
> —*Victoria Bailey*

Although clearly not in a manifesto mood, Brandon and Victoria had fun playing with contradiction and surprise. Nobody wants to notice a dead bird falling but carcasses exist among flowers, and to notice them is to acknowledge the life lived. When Victoria writes that "People watch TV when it's not on," she is commenting upon that favorite American pastime.

In the poem "Unholy Missions," Kaufman writes:

> I want to prove that Los Angeles is a practical joke played on us by superior beings on a humorous planet.

This wild poem gave me the idea of immersing my seventh graders in the fun of being outrageous. In fact they had a little too much fun, inventing intrigue among teachers and school officials, as well as making up terrible things about their friends. The truly offensive statements (even with names changed to protect the guilty) have been vaporized from the following collaborative list poem:

> I want to prove that the Loch Ness Monster hides out in my basement

> I want to prove that glue is not what we ate as children

> I want to prove that the sun is actually an astronaut with gas

> I want to prove that school lunch is actually leftover military food

> I want to prove that Tupac Shakur is still alive and faked his own death to escape the East Coast, West Coast battle

> I want to prove that wind is screaming souls that are lost

> I want to prove that Satan sent some of his angels to be principals

> I want to prove that books are alive

> I want to sue my mother for false advertising saying that I was a beautiful child

> I want to prove that video games are not mind-controlling zombies but educational devices to teach people that every time you jump you hear a "boing"

> I want to prove that school is a daytime jail for students

> I want to prove that those we feel are retarded are really geniuses

> I want to prove that Cocoa Puffs come from the stars

I want to expose Tropicana for making a lethal drink: O.J.

I want to prove that the Statue of Liberty is actually a crazy bum who froze outside

I want to prove that snow comes from the macaroni and cheese God is using to make lasagna

I want to prove that teachers give homework so kids won't have a social life

I want to prove that our dreams are spirits in another dimension

I want to prove that heaven is globs of Cool-Whip

I want to prove that grandparents all over the world have an organization called The Cheek Pinchers

I want to prove that chocolate is diarrhea from the angels

I want to put an end to the use of unnecessary letters in words

I want to prove that we travel from planet to planet unknowingly

I want to prove that stars are the eyes of my family looking down on me

I want to prove that uniforms are invented to put children in a world of drabness to make their brain cells bored; therefore they can't act up

Sarcasm in satire is empowering, especially in middle school. Those holy terrors with tongues firmly implanted in cheeks learned to dish the insults as well as take them. With the empathy of sages, the contemplativeness of philosophers, and the wit of satirists, these writers have more in common with Bob Kaufman than simply being music lovers "of color." In Kaufman, they have discovered a kindred soul, someone never too grown up, someone "all the way live" even when it hurts.

Bibliography

Kaufman, Bob. *The Ancient Rain*. New York: New Directions, 1981.

———. *Cranial Guitar*. Minneapolis: Coffee House, 1996.

———. *Golden Sardine*. San Francisco: City Lights, 1967.

———. *Solitudes Crowded with Loneliness*. New York: New Directions, 1965.

AURELIA LUCÍA HENRIQUEZ

Be-Bop-Bo-Duh

Writing Jazz Poetry

BOOKER T. WASHINGTON, the powerful and influential African American "Wizard of Tuskegee," once said, "The first thing to do is to get into every school, private, public, or otherwise, Negro literature and history. We aren't trying to displace other literature, but trying to acquaint all children with Negro history and literature." Throughout high school and college, it had been my desire to incorporate the history and literature of all peoples into the school curriculum. Being of Native American and Latino heritage, I know the importance of one's cultural history. My grandmother always said, "Our stories are our only true source of the history of our people. Our words are the heart of our people. The youth of today must learn all of these stories in our own words, and then maybe they'll be able to understand the Native way." Very early in life, I began to see "our stories" as mirror images of interpersonal relations within society. More importantly, I understood why my grandmother often acquainted young people with a cherished piece of pottery, a hand-made wedding basket, or a religious ritual. Our literature has the power to create and recreate, again and again, the most important cultural values and therefore the history of the group that produced it.

Recently I had the opportunity to teach a course called "One Country: Many Cultures" for the Brentwood School District in Long Island, N.Y., a district whose student population is an exquisite prismatic sunbow of cultures and races. The course encompassed literature from the Harlem Renaissance era, Latino heritage, and Native American cultures. My aim was to use poetry to go as deeply as possible into these cultures. My students ranged from eleven to fourteen years old. (I also used some of the same lessons with my regular third grade class.)

In this unit, I tried to show my students a connection between poetry and music. Many of my older students were very much aware of the strong presence of poetry in rap music, but I also wanted them to see and hear music—jazz, in particular—in poetry. My approach involved my students in language that embodies the sounds of everyday life and of music: the language of onomatopoeia.

We began with the Jazz Era. The class devoted approximately two weeks to becoming familiar with this period. Together we read books such as *The First Book of Jazz* by Langston Hughes and *Jazz: My Music, My People* by Morgan Monceaux, two resources I've found to be excellent for both my older and younger students. In the foreword to *Jazz: My Music, My People*, Wynton Marsalis wrote, "They say that in order to know the real meaning of a thing you must go back to the beginning," words of wisdom I emphasized to my students. And so we read and talked about the birth of jazz. I wanted my students to understand that jazz grew out of the beating of African drums (*the* basic rhythm instrument) and that jazz began with individuals playing for fun, in the South. I also wanted them to become familiar with various jazz instruments.

As a first step toward this, we reread Hughes's discussion of jazz instruments. Then the class created a semantic map based on jazz music. I simply wrote the word *JAZZ* in a large rectangle on the chalkboard. The students drew arrows from the box, at the ends of which they wrote the names and drew pictures of the jazz instruments they had read about. (The words became next week's spelling work.) The students enjoyed making the map. Of course some of them were already quite familiar with the instruments, which they played in band or music class. Others were able to offer information about the jazz instruments used in salsa and merengue (bongos, claves, guiros, calabashes, maracas, etc.) Prior to this lesson, I had gathered many musical instruments, which I now displayed at the front of the room. The children and I demonstrated how each instrument is played.

To begin the writing part, I wrote the word *onomatopoeia* on the board and read it aloud. My students loved saying this word. They found it very amusing. I said, "If you think that saying this strange word is fun, just wait until you begin writing some onomatopoeic words." I explained that onomatopoeic words are those that imitate sounds. To clarify, I had various students come to the board. When I said the name of a thing, they had to write down the sound it makes. I told them to think of it as a game.

When I said "gun," the student wrote *bang*. And so it went, with *water/splash, bee/buzz, train/choo choo, snake/hiss,* etc. The game was not only fun, it gave students a better feel for the concept at hand. For me, it was interesting to see how students responded to and interpreted the sounds of various nouns.

Now that the students had learned about jazz and onomatopoeia, they were ready to see examples of jazz poetry. We had delved into the poems of Langston Hughes many times before, but this time I wanted them to see him in a new light, as jazz poet, so I selected poems that illustrated him as a "composer" as well as a writer. Some of the children's favorite jazz poems of his were "Children's Rhymes," "Juke Box Love Song," "Ladies' Boogie," "Life Is Fine," "Dream Boogie," and "Jam Session." However, our all-time favorite was his "Song for a Banjo Dance." Some students felt that it needed to be set to music, but others argued that it didn't need any music, because it created its own!

Finally, before we began to write, I provided an example of a poem that clearly uses onomatopoeia, "Black Dance" by Luis Pales Matos:

Black Dance

Calabó[1] and bamboo,
Bamboo and calabó.
The great Cocoroco[2] says: tu-cu-tu
The great Cocoroca[3] says: to-co-tó
It is the iron sun that burns in Timbuctu.
It is the Black dance of Fernando Poo.
The pig in the mud squeals: pru-pru-prú.
The toad in the pond dreams: cro-cro-cró.
Calabó and bamboo,
Bamboo and calabó.

The junjunes[4] break out in a furious ú.
The gongos[5] quiver with a profound ó.
It's the Black race that is undulating
with the rhythm of the mariyandá.[6]

---

1. African wood for drums
2. Main African tribal chief
3. Cocoroco's wife
4. Rudimentary violins
5. Drums
6. Black dance in Puerto Rico

The botucos[7] already arrive at the fiesta.
Dancing and dancing the Negress gives in.
Calabó and bamboo,
Bamboo and calabó.

The great Cocoroco says: tu-cu-tu.
The great Cocoroca says: to-co-tó.

Red-islands pass, islands of shoeblack:
Haiti, Martinique, Congo, Camaroon:
The papiamento[8] Antilles of rum
and the patois islands of the volcano,
which in the grave sound
of song give in.

Calabó and bamboo,
Bamboo and calabó.
It is the iron sun that burns in Timbuctu.
It is the Black dance of Fernando Poo.
The African soul that is vibrating
in the thick rhythm of mariyandá.

Calabó and bamboo,
Bamboo and calabó.
The great Cocoroco says: tu-cu-tu.
The great Cocoroca says: to-co-tó.

I presented the poem in English, as I found it it, in Maria Teresa Babin's book *Borinquen,* because the onomatpoeia comes through quite clearly. I felt that Matos had to be included in our exploration of African American poetry because of all Puerto Rican poets, he is the most famous for celebrating the African heritage in Puerto Rico. The children enjoyed the onomatopoeic sounds in his poem. My younger students especially enjoyed dramatizing this poem and imitating its sounds. Many students saw that Matos's use of onomatopoeia helped to provide a verbal picture of the Puerto Rican landscape. We also talked about how Matos's poem expressed the joy and power of blacks in Puerto Rico, whereas many of Hughes's poems celebrating blackness had the cloud of American racism hanging over them.

---

7. Minor chieftains
8. Caribbean dialect of Curaçao

At this point the students were quite enthusiastic about writing their own poems using onomatopoeic words. I turned off the lights and told the students to put their heads down, eyes closed. When the room was silent, I said that we were about to travel backward in time to see "Satchmo" Louis Armstrong live! I raised the volume on my compact disk player and played his versions of "Cabaret," "Do You Know What It Means to Miss New Orleans," "Someday," and "Hello, Dolly."

I was elated to see my students' hands and feet begin tapping and their heads bobbing, as they began singing the refrains. I knew it was the time to write. Here are some examples of what the students wrote:

(Piano) Ting, Tin, Tang!
(Sax) Tow, Tow, Tum!
(Trumpet) Braw, Brum, Brah, Brum!
(Drum) Tee, Tee, Tah, Tah, Tee!
(Singer) Skee-dee-daddle-doodle-dee-dah-dah-dop!

    —Amanda Carlo

I was listening to a jazz band and I heard the trumpet player play:
BRUNH
BRUNH
BRUNH
BARAM
I was watching a jazz band and I heard the banjo players play:
TING
PING
PLINK
PLUNK
And I heard a smooth cat scattin a tune:
BE-BOP-BO-DUH-DO-DO-LOW-DO
DUH-DO-DUH-DO-DO-DODDLE-DEE!
I was watching and listening to all the people saying:
YEAH!
YEAH!
YES!
YEAH!
JAZZ!

    —Alicia Casieri

At a BIG BAND STREET PARADE
Louie played his SINGING GOLDEN TRUMPET:
BRAHN-BAA-BA-BAUNN!
Yeah, his cats played a MEAN DEEP BASS:
HUMM-BUM-BA-BUM-HUMM!
And a BAD DRUM: DOOM-BAM-BOOM!
All the young second liners just DANCIN down the street
In a BIG BAND PARADE!

  —Yesenia Portillo

Afterward, I grouped students in response teams. They read their poems aloud in these peer groups, with special attention to the onomatopoeic words, and, using suggestions from their classmates, revised their poems. Then they checked for spelling and punctuation.

In the words of Morgan Monceaux, "Jazz is an oral tradition—it's like storytelling. One person hears something and passes it on." I wanted to continue this oral tradition. Just as Buddy Bolden influenced Louis Armstrong and through him Dizzy Gillespie and Miles Davis, we as teachers have the chance to be future-makers or future-breakers. Through us, our students see where they've been and take on the confidence to know where they're going. My intention was to imbue my students with the spirit and challenge of the music of the jazz era and the poetry of the Harlem Renaissance. Most important, I wanted to stimulate them to write with pleasure and creativity.

Bibliography

Babin, Maria Teresa. *Borinquen.* New York: Knopf, 1974.

Hughes, Langston. *The First Book of Jazz.* New York: Franklin Watts, 1955.

———. *Selected Poems.* New York: Random House, 1959.

Monceaux, Morgan. *Jazz: My Music, My People* (New York: Knopf, 1994).

M ELBA J OYCE B OYD

The Music in Afroamerican Poetry

UNLIKE MOST western literary traditions, which have become more bound to visual imagery and silenced through print, Afroamerican poetry has maintained its musical heritage and expanded the aural dimensions of the page. The deepest messages of Afroamerican poetry are embedded in the very sounds and rhythms of the words. Though strongly influenced by English and American literature, Afroamerican poetry is distinguished as a poetry that must be spoken to be fully realized.

In their written verse, Afroamerican poets have consciously emulated the dynamics of song. The translation of song to poetic form involves contrast and comparison, repetition and refrain, sarcasm, and hyperbole, which are characteristics of Africanity. The African musical scale is apparent in the elliptical rhyme schemes and asymmetrical patterns of vowel sounds and internal rhymes of Afroamerican poetry. Variations in line length also contribute to shifts in rhythm and perspective. All these constructions depend on aural interpretation. Ultimately, freedom is the ideological subtext of this creative structure.

Africanity, in the case of the ballad, often includes "call and response" in the refrain, continuing the African tradition and foreshadowing the blues. The lead singer calls for a response in the refrain it interfaces, using an explicit question or implicit suggestion. In contrast to the British ballad form, the Afroamerican tradition includes audience involvement throughout the poem; also, the lines of the caller can be extended by improvisation. Of course involvement occurs in the silent reading of a poem as well, but the printed page tends to confine the poem by fixing the words in place.

Rap, which also relies on improvisation, evolved from the black oral tradition as well. Its roots can be traced past urban street corners, rural juke joints, slave quarters, and beyond the Atlantic Ocean to the

African griots. Poems composed during slavery, such as "Wild Negro Bill," are the earliest examples of Afroamerican oral poetry. These poems use wit and hyperbole to expose the tyranny of slavery. Creative improvisation heightens one's enjoyment of the poem as each orator adds or alters the presentation. No folk poem is etched in stone.

"Wild Negro Bill" uses the collective "I" to engage the spirit of the rebellious slave in everyone. The speaker embodies the voice of the male folk hero as he assumes the identity of Wild Bill and brags that he has never worked, "an' I never will." By assuming the character of Wild Bill, the speaker symbolically overcomes slavery by becoming a superman. The seriousness of the subject, including killing the overseer and living as a fugitive, is vicariously liberating. Hyperbole contributes to the humor in the poem, as "Wild Negro Bill" performs superhuman feats with exuberance and imagination:

> I'se wild Nigger Bill
> Frum Redpepper Hill.
> I never did wo'k an' I never will.
>
> I'se done killed de Boss.
> I'se knocked down de hoss.
> I eats up raw goose widout apple sauce!
>
> I'se run-a-way Bill,
> I knows dey mought kill;
> But ole Mosser hain't cotch me, an' he never will!

This type of testimonial returns in new adventures of "Wild Bill" by the twentieth-century poet Sterling Brown. Other folk poems about "Slim" and "Shine," improvised and later published by Sterling Brown and Etheridge Knight, demonstrate how unsung folk heroes champion the spirit of freedom well into the twentieth century. Brown's "Slim" appears in the following excerpt:

> St. Peter said, "Well,
>   you got back quick,
> How's de devil? An what's
>   He's latest trick?"
>
> An' Slim say, "Peter,
>   I really cain't tell,
> The place was Dixie
>   That I took for hell."

Then Peter say, "You must
    Be crazy, I vow,
Where'n hell dja think Hell was,
    Any how?

"Git on back to de yearth,
    Cause I got de fear
You'se a leetle too dumb,
    Fo' to stay up here."

He returns in Etheridge Knight's "Shine and the Titanic":

And, yeah, brothers
while white/america sings about the unsink
able molly brown
(who was hustling the titanic
when it went down)
 I sing to thee of Shine
the stoker who was hip
enough to flee the fucking ship
and let the white folks drown
with screams on their lips
(jumped his black ass into the dark sea, Shine did,
broke free from the straining steel.
yeah, I sing of Shine

The Poetry of the Blues

Published in the 1980s, Jayne Cortez's poem, "You Know (For the People Who Speak the You Know Language)," not only extends the blues and the ongoing influence of the oral tradition of poetry, but also speaks to the complex socioeconomic reality that underpins the music and explains why that reality is integral to Afroamerican creative expression:

    You know
I sure would like to write a blues
    you know
a good feeling piece to my writing hand
    you know
my hand that can bring two pieces of life
together in your ear
    you know

one drop of blues turning a paper clip
into three wings and a bone into a revolt
    you know
a blues passing up the stereotype symbols
    you know
go into the dark meat loaf a crocodile and pin point the process
    you know
into a solo a hundred times like the first line of Aretha Franklin
    you know
like Big Mama Thornton
    you know
I sure would like to write a blues
    you know

The printed page cannot convey the full effect of the vortex of Jayne Cortez's imagery. In fact, one should hear Cortez reading on her album "Spitfire," made with Ornette Coleman, to experience her work's aural power. And yet even on the page her work has the decidedly oral dimensions of jazz poetry. Her lines roll from beginning to end without hesitating for a comma. The unpunctuated rhythm is generated from aggregates of recurring images. She constructs thematic constellations that explode and interact on several planes simultaneously. The rhythm is controlled by line space, repetition, refrain, and the intensity of moral conflict infused in the imagery. Her poem "I Am New York" demonstrates a similar structural control in its reiteration of the theme of urban crisis, reinforced by verbal moves attuned to spontaneity and surprise:

i am new york city
here is my brain of hot sauce
my tobacco teeth my
    mattress of bedbug tongue
legs apart   hand on chin
    war on the roof   insults
pointed fingers   pushcarts
my contraceptives all

look at my pelvis blushing

I am new york city of blood
police and fried pies
I rub my docks red with grenadine
and jelly madness in a flow of tokay

my huge skull of pigeons
my seance of peeping toms
my plaited ovaries excuse me
this is my grime my thigh of
steelspoons and toothpicks
i imitate no one

The connections between folk, rap, and jazz poems demonstrate the continuity of Africanity and the creative consciousness that continues this literary tradition. The writing exercises that follow provide ways for students to experience that tradition for themselves.

Writing Exercises

The following exercises are directly related to the previous discussion and include examples drawn from it.

I. "Wild Negro Bill" is a folk poem that demonstrates both the entertainment value of oral poetry and its sometimes very serious messages.

A. Copy the lines of the poem "Wild Negro Bill."

B. Repeat the refrain in a second stanza and add new lines that represent new adventures for the persona. The lines may vary from the original arrangement, but should maintain the overall meter of the poem.

II. Select a popular rap song and write down the lyrics.

A. Arrange the line lengths according to the rapper's pauses. Count the syllables and beats in each line. By timing the delivery of each line, you can measure the difference between the number of syllables and how long the rapper lingers on each word.

B. Write an additional stanza for the rap, keeping the pace, the meter, and the beat of the original song.

C. Decode the lyrics of a rap song. Translate the words into standard English and see what kind of poem you can make with this new version.

III. Select a folk poem, such as "Wild Negro Bill," then select a literary poem that imitates a folk form, such as Sterling Brown's "Slim in Hell" (you can find examples in anthologies such as *The Norton Anthology of African American Literature*). Discuss how both the folk poem and the literary folk poem use exaggeration, sarcasm, and symbolism to express a theme. Then:

A. Write a parody of "Slim in Hell" as "Slim in the Ghetto" or a parody of "But He Was Cool or: He Even Stopped for Green Lights" by Haki Madhubuti (Don L. Lee) as "But He Was a Mack."

B. Write a poem that uses "call and response" as a basic part of the form. For an example of the format, refer to Frances E. W. Harper's "A Double Standard" or to one of the folk poems or spirituals. Here is an excerpt from Harper's "A Double Standard":

> Do you blame me that I loved him?
>   If when standing all alone
> I cried for bread a careless world
>   Pressed to my lips a stone.
>
> Do you blame me that I loved him,
>   that my heart beat glad and free,
> When he told me in the sweetest tones
>   He loved but only me?
>
> Can you blame me that I did not see
>   Beneath his burning kiss
> The serpent's wiles, nor even hear
>   The deadly adder hiss?
>
> Can you blame me that my heart grew cold
>   That the tempted, tempter turned;
> When he was feted and caressed
>   And I was coldly spurned?
>
> Would you blame him, when you draw from me
>   Your dainty robes aside.
> If he with gilded baits should claim
>   Your fairest for his bride?
>
> Would you blame the world if it should press
>   On him a civic crown;
> And see me struggling in the depth
>   Then harshly press me down?

IV. In writing a blues poem, such as Jayne Cortez's "You Know," you need a refrain and a series of verses that construct a rhythm pattern. To write a blues poem:

    A. Establish a refrain.

    B. Decide on a theme and free-associate images related to it.

    C. Regulate your rhythm pattern by counting the number of beats and/or syllables in a line and pauses.

V. Write a jazz poem while listening to a jazz composition.

    A. Determine the theme of your poem.

    B. Associate and connect images by using verbs to expand the images into a broader concept.

    C. Use sound as a method of punctuation. In other words, instead of commas and periods, use the line length and clusters of words to begin and end an idea or an image.

Conclusion

The music in Afroamerican poetry demonstrates how sound itself carries meaning, and how that poetry revels in humor, hope, and vigilance in the face of incredible difficulties, shaping meaning out of chaos. Afroamerican poetry has retained the power of song, because song retains the heartbeat of the culture.

Bibliography

Cortez, Jayne. *Coagulations.* New York: Thunder's Mouth Press, 1984.

Gates, Henry Louis, Jr., Nellie Y. McKay, and others, eds. *Norton Anthology of African American Literature.* New York: W. W. Norton, 1997.

Harper, Frances E. W. *The Brighter Coming Day.* Frances Foster, ed. New York: The Feminist Press, 1989.

Randall, Dudley, ed. *The Black Poets.* New York: Bantam, 1971. Randall's anthology includes the poems by Sterling Brown and Etheridge Knight discussed in this essay.

MARK STATMAN

Hidden Beauty, Willful Craziness

Teaching Poems by Jayne Cortez and Lucille Clifton

Under the Edge of February

Under the edge of february
in hawk of a throat
hidden by ravines of sweet oil
by temples of switch blades
beautiful in its sound of fertility
beautiful in its turban of funeral crepe
beautiful in its camouflage of grief
in its solitude of bruises
in its arson of alert
Who will enter its beautiful calligraphy of blood

Its beautiful mask of fish net
mask of hubcap mask of ice picks mask
of watermelon rinds mask of umbilical cords
changing into a mask of rubber bands
Who will enter this beautiful beautiful mask of
punctured bladders moving with a mask of chapsticks

Compound of Hearts   Compound of Hearts

Where is the lucky number for this shy love
this top heavy beauty bathed with charcoal water
self conscious against a mosaic of broken bottles
broken locks broken pipes broken
bloods of broken spirits broken through like
broken promises

Landlords   Junkies   Thieves
enthroning themselves in you
they burn up couches they burn down houses
and infuse themselves against memory

every thought
a pavement of old belts
every performance
a ceremonial pick up
how many more orphans   how many neglected shrines
how many more stolen feet   stolen guns
stolen watch bands of death
in you how many times

Harlem

hidden by ravines of sweet oil
by temples of switch blades
beautiful in your sound of fertility
beautiful in your turban of funeral crepe
beautiful in your camouflage of grief
in your solitude of bruises in
your arson of alert
beautiful

Whenever I've taught this poem by Jayne Cortez (usually with ten-to fourteen-year-olds), I've always been surprised by how willing the students are to tackle the poem's complexities: its harsh descriptions of urban life, its anger, and its notion—serious and ironic—of what, in all this chaos, is beautiful. Cortez's ideas about beauty often frame our conversations. Most students are not used to thinking about beauty as something that isn't obvious, something that can be hidden. They're not used to taking images or ideas that are ostensibly "ugly" and thinking of them as beautiful in another context.

To get students thinking in this direction, I ask them to think about what "beauty" means, what they mean when they call something "beautiful." Their initital responses are often conventional: from nature—flowers, a meadow, sun, stars, moon; from the urban—gleaming skyscrapers, glittering night streets, well-dressed people strolling; from people—those nice clothes again, muscular men, slim women, implications of good times.

A natural response to what Cortez describes is to look away. But Cortez demands the opposite: she wants us to look and to look hard. So where in the poem, I'll ask the students, given what they've described as beautiful, is the beauty? The poem is full of sadness and grief ("broken / bloods of broken spirits broken through like / broken promises"), violence ("they burn up couches they burn down houses"), garbage ("mask of hubcaps mask of ice picks mask / of watermelon rinds mask of umbilical cords"). It's a poem of anger. And yet, Cortez insistently speaks about the beauty. How? Why?

As the students think about the poem and my questions, I'll begin to discuss other possible conceptions of beauty, where else we can see it and of the possibility of beauty growing out of what we might also think of as "ugliness." For example, they've all seen rainbow oil sheen in puddles on the street. Many know about the spectacular effects air pollution has on sunsets. I'll talk about London's mysterious, evocative fog of previous decades and its ordinary origins in coal smoke. I'll mention Monet's paintings of the Seine, where the magnificent colorations he depicts are actually a reflection of the river's pollution, as well as the excitement of the billowing smoke in his railroad station paintings. I'll talk about spiders spinning their gorgeous webs as a way to trap and kill. I'll even bring up ambergris, which I'll describe as "whale vomit," and how it is used in making fine perfumes. We'll come up with examples of destructive beauty: hurricanes, tornadoes, volcanoes. Great structures like pyramids and sphinxes built by slaves. We'll talk about perspective, how some people find things beautiful and others can't see them, how this happens with art, poetry, clothes, music, weather. Finally we'll return to "Under the Edge of February." "What's beautiful here?" I'll ask again.

At this point, we're able to read new things in the Cortez poem. We can talk about the action in the poem, the characters in it, the setting. I've taught this poem in different places, but when I teach it in New York City schools, the students will always relate it to their own neighborhoods. They think about their streets, the people they know, their own lives. We talk not just about what they see, but what they know about what they see. The students' comments become both intensely observant and personal. They often remark on the fact that where they live is home: whatever the limitations, their neighborhoods are important to them. These are places where my students have friends, where they've played and been happy. They'll talk about the life of where they live: the sounds and smells, people walking on the streets and hanging out in groups talking, the fact of people's homes being here, that there are people eating, sleeping, dreaming.

My students also respond to the "negatives" of Cortez's poem, particularly the problems of outsiders misreading and misunderstanding the world they know. We'll discuss the problems of public perception arising from skewed media depictions: that newspapers, television, and movies show one side of where they live (the crime and the violence, the poverty), and not the other side (schools, stores, churches, homes, the community). In other words, the not-so-obvious, the hidden in Cortez's "beautiful." When we've reached this point in the discussion, we're also at the starting point for their writing: I ask the students to respond to Cortez's poem by writing their own poems to, of, for, and about beauty, and where they find it.

Poem

Blue is cool
I found it in the sky
in the ocean, on pottery

Red is hot
I found it in the sun
the rainbow
on flowers, the outside of a building
on clothes

White is delicate
I found it in the clouds
in the classroom
in my house
on flowers
inside and outside buildings
on dogs

—*Regina Smith, seventh grade*

Dreamer

Once I had a dream
I could see all the places of the world
In my mind I could see
Japan, Russia, Germany
All the people wanted to sleep

and sleep on
Their sleep
seemed very beautiful to them
All I could see everywhere
was people with eyes
closed

      —Tara Thomas, eighth grade

It's winter in the morning
It's snowing
It's snowing white big flakes
Cars are covered with snow
Too many accidents
People are falling down
Breaking legs
Cars lose control of their breaks
There is no service
Cars hitting people
People bleeding through everywhere
Snow is getting red
Because of the bleeding
Of the person who had the big accident
Too many people are dying
This weather's got to change
This weather is cold below

      —Francisco Rodriguez, sixth grade

Night

It was night
and it was 9:00
and I'm flying in the sky
and I can see the North Star
Some people are watching "The Jeffersons"
Some people are watching "Jeopardy"
There are people doing exercise
There is a person riding a bike in the street
I went to sit on a tree branch
It broke
I fell on a van
and hurt my back

and then I flew
I saw the Statue of Liberty
It is so beautiful
I saw the ocean
The world is so beautiful
I saw Broadway
The lights look wonderful
I can see people
The people are doing their show

  —Charisse Robinson, fifth grade

Beauty

The feeling of beauty
It's like
  falling in
Love
  Diamonds
Jewelry
  It is such a good feeling
You feel like getting
Married
  In a
White clean
  Crystal
    Dress
Your hair
  long and
beautiful
  The water in the Dominican
Republic
  Crystal clean
The streets clean
No, no dirt, dust
  mud
but beauty
like
  Romeo and Juliet
  Adam and Eve
Emotions of a
  Dream

Love
Fantasy
It feels so real
having Beauty
But dream love fantasy
is all it is in this
Dirty World

     —Jeanette Cortijo, eighth grade

It is black but the white
freckles of the stars stand out
I am blind but I can still
see the shining light of the
moon standing out in the
night
I am a person but
to the creatures that lurk
beyond I am prey
I look and listen
but there is nothing
nothing to see or hear
the sounds of
a furious river
the shadows of
a soundless bird
shows in the moon light
I think of what humans
are
doing to the silent and
peaceful land
the animals, not mean but
nice
in a strange way
I was glad that we hadn't
destroyed it all
Yet I had to go back
this was not my home
my home was in the smog of
technology

     —Jason Ozner, sixth grade

What Is Beauty

A cold January night
What happens at night
All the killing
All the shots in the wall
All the drugs in the world
Is this beauty?
Beauty.
I'll tell you
about Beauty
What is good
Beauty is real
That's Beauty
What about living,
is that Beauty?
I know it is for me
All the beauty in the world
is what I am living for
I know that's what I am
living for

—*Shantel Bumpurs, fifth grade*

Happiest

I was walking down
the street
I heard a noise and
I was looking
for it and I could
not see it
and thought it was
a cat
but when I saw
that it was
not a cat I saw
something big
it was bigger
than a cat and then
I thought it was a
dog but it
was not a dog
and when I saw it
was a poor man I

gave the person $20
because I was not
happy that
he lived in the
street so I
was going to take
him to a shelter
and he was hidden
because he was
afraid and when
I saw his face
he did look like
good people but
he looked like
a child and the
child was hidden
the man went to the
shelter and he
had a good life
and house

> —*Jose Martinez, fifth grade*

▶   ▶   ▶

If one way to read Jayne Cortez's poem is to look for not-so-obvious beauty, Lucille Clifton's poem "roots" is about the announcement of beauty, not necessarily as something we observe, but as something we *assume*: our beauty is in our character, it is active, about one's self, and the identification of that self with a kind of spirituality that reflects hope and possibility about the way life ought to be. This is a poem I often teach after having taught "Under the Edge of February." I like how they stand with and against each other: Cortez's explosive barrage of images, her intense language, followed by Clifton's language much more simple and direct, yet no less complex in its drive to think about the lives we lead.

roots

call it our craziness even,
call it anything.
it is the life thing in us
that will not let us die.
even in death's hand

we fold the fingers up
and call them greens and
grow on them,
we hum them and make music.
call it our wildness then,
we are lost from the field
of flowers, we become
a field of flowers.
call it our craziness
our wildness
call it our roots,
it is the light in us
it is the light of us
it is the light, call it
whatever you have to,
call it anything.*

My students are often initially quite puzzled by the poem—what is she talking about? What does she mean by "the light," what does she mean about death, what is this thing of becoming the field? Although the Cortez poem is much longer and much more detailed, the immediacy of the details, coupled with forcefulness of the long lines and the repetition, helps the students to enter the world of the poem. But Lucille Clifton's seeming simplicity confuses them.

To help them, I'll ask the students to think about themselves: "What makes each one of you who you are? What makes you different, not just from the person sitting next to you, but different from the person you've been?" They find it easy to talk about this: physical growth, personality development. They know how much has changed in their lives. But I'll then ask: "What do you think makes you the same person now that you were five years ago, ten years ago? What makes you the person you've always been?"

Sometimes this is hard. For many, these are odd questions because this kind of self-analysis is unfamiliar and difficult terrain for them. They'll note certain kinds of things: "I've always liked pizza but I haven't always liked basketball, before I just liked to run. I couldn't read

---

* I'm grateful to my friend and colleague, writer and teacher Christian McEwen, for introducing me to this poem.

before, but I always liked when someone read me books. I used to like 'Sesame Street' but now I prefer horror films." But students quickly see that none of these things, while perhaps significant, is essential to their lives. But the initial thinking about such significant things can help them, through deeper analytical thinking, to see other, more essential sides of themselves: they can figure out that basketball and running demonstrate a need or desire for movement, activity, play with others, friendships. Pizza translates into the need or desire for food pleasure, for enjoyment. Books, whether read by or to them, suggest a growing desire to learn, to imagine, to know about the world they live in. The very fact that the children are changing often leads them to conclude that change itself is a necessary constant. As we continue to talk about the important things in their lives and figure out why those things have meaning, the students are able to see much more clearly the whys behind what they know about themselves; they are able to see constants in their thoughts and emotions, in their creating and dreaming.

Sometimes the students and I will venture into the notion of the spirit and the spiritual. They'll get the connection between the spirit (sometimes they'll call it soul) and Clifton's "light," the "life thing in us / that will not let us die." We'll contrast this with her image of "death's hand," noting that—if Clifton is right—if we cannot die, then death is not something to be afraid of. The hand might extend itself, but we can fold its fingers up, and take control of death. The green that death becomes is about renewal, the humming about joy. For Clifton, the life thing that is in us, that is us, the craziness and wildness, is so powerful that even when we think we are lost, it's only a matter of perspective. You are not lost from the field if you allow yourself to become part, because, as part of the field, you'll know exactly where you are (I think of Wallace Stevens's idea that to understand the snow and ice and the snowman, we must have a "mind of winter.")

Finally, I'll ask my students why the poem is called "roots." Their answers vary but they are all related to a single idea—that roots nourish us, they keep us grounded, allow us to live. The craziness Clifton speaks of in the poem is not madness, but fearless excitement, willful ecstasy. Being rooted in the earth means that craziness and wildness need not be aimless and destructive because, as with the "we" and "our" of the poem, Clifton means they are part of history, family, and community.

Before my students begin to write, I'll sometimes read them another Lucille Clifton poem, "new bones":

new bones

we will wear
new bones again.
we will leave
these rainy days,
break out through
another mouth
into sun and honey time.
worlds buzz over us like bees,
we be splendid in new bones.
other people think they know
how long life is
how strong life is.
we know.

To begin a discussion, I'll talk about Clifton's certainty that there are things others may think they know, but which we know we know. I'll ask them to think about things in life that seem absolutely real and certain to them and to think how that certainty might give them "roots"—just as Clifton's confidence comes so much from her own sense of that light inside. What would they call their roots? What is their light? What runs with them, sings with them and in them? I'll ask them to think about their own ideas of what is possible for the world and for them. To describe their own lives, what words could they use?

I am born as I get
to see nature
flowers blooming I nature
is in my hand
as I see the
earth start
to
spin as I feel it in my
soul as I admire myself as it is
a picture of myself as
I am going to live or
die as
I feel the sun bursting
on me as I am myself

I start
to
grow as God is
talking to me don't
fear if death
I am
here
with you
As I talk to
myself
I feel in my blood as
I feel healthy not sick
as nature is
blowing away until I
listen to what
they are
saying as
beams feel
like they
are taking me to heaven
or hell as I get scared
I feel haunted but
I get a family. As
I feel in my mind
as I sing to myself
as I celebrate because
I had parents
as it never ends
as it shines
to heaven as
there is no such
thing of hell as they bring me
for as my soul stays gold as
God stays I am myself

    —*Chris DeMeglio, sixth grade*

who are you?
what are you?
the moon and
the stars
roots go with me
everywhere

I breathe it
I see it
what are roots?

      —*Aracelis Roman, fifth grade*

Call me

Call me sweet
call me friendly
call me pretty
but do not call
me ugly

because you will
see me get ugly
very ugly and you will
not want to see me
again

      —*Sophia Negron, fifth grade*

I have sunshine each and every day
      but as I focus out my window
            sick from the cold weather
I can feel my solemn soul
      translating through my body
      a tear falls from my dark
           brown eyes
When I start to cry my fulfilling
      angels tell me to fulfill
           my happiness

      —*Erica Hardaway, fifth grade*

Bones to Our Roots

Bones by day roots by
night, you think you
know when it is night
you think you know not
to fight. But you don't
know and I don't know
when we will die, we

could die right now.
One day when you
and I die we will
walk in a field of flowers
and dream about day and
night, think about when to
fight. Maybe we will
come back in a new
form and we will still
dream about day and
night.

> —*Mikel Murray, fifth grade*

Good-bye

Good-bye to you
I will be back
I promise I will
I will not be gone as long as the universe exists or as long as the air is here
Remember
my living soul will always be with you when I'm gone
I will come back through the light
say hello
touch your hand

> —*Michael Schiralli, sixth grade*

Bibliography

Clifton, Lucille. *good woman: poems and a memoir, 1969–1980*. Brockport, N.Y.: BOA Editions, 1987.

Stetson, Erlene, ed. *Black Sister: Poetry from Black American Women, 1746–1980*. Bloomington, Ind.: Indiana University Press, 1981.

Ron Padgett

Say the Word

Using the Poetry of Aimé Césaire

WHEN PEOPLE REFER to African American writers, we usually assume they mean black writers of the United States, forgetting that the
Americas are plural. Thus we overlook writers of African descent such
as René Depestre of Haiti, Léon Damas of French Guiana, and Aimé
Césaire of Martinique, all of whom have influenced the course of black
literature around the world.

Of these three, Césaire's influence has been the most pervasive. His
long poem, *Notebook of a Return to the Native Land*, written in 1938,
served as a sort of manifesto for Negritude, which eventually became
the first global movement of black culture and literature. In fact he
coined the term *negritude*. Blending surrealism and the history, landscape, and culture of Martinique, Césaire's poetry comes at the reader
like a series of lush explosions, sometimes angry, sometimes lyrical, but
always charged with energy and mystery.

In fact, most of his poems are so mysterious that teachers are
stumped as to how to use them to inspire student writing. One poem,
though, offers a clear possibility:

Word

         Within me
from myself
to myself
outside any constellation
clenched in my hands only
this rare hiccup of an ultimate raving spasm
keep vibrating word

         I will have luck outside the labyrinth
longer wider keep vibrating
in tighter and tighter waves
in a lasso to catch me
in a rope to hang me

and let me be nailed by all the arrows
and their bitterest curare
to the beautiful center stake of very cool stars

vibrate
vibrate you very essence of the dark
in a wing in a throat from so much perishing
the word nigger
emerged fully armed from the howling
of a poisonous flower
the word nigger
all filthy with parasites
the word nigger
loaded with roaming bandits

with screaming mothers
crying children
a sizzling of flesh and horny matter
burning, acrid
the word nigger
like the sun bleeding from its claw
onto the sidewalk of clouds
the word nigger
like the last laugh calved by innocence
between the tiger's fangs
and as the word sun is a ringing of bullets
and the word night a ripping of taffeta
the word nigger
          dense, right?
from the thunder of a summer
    appropriated by
             incredulous liberties

    —Translated by Clayton Eshleman and Annette Smith

In this poem filled with exhaltation and rage, Césaire talks to a word that for him has a violent fascination, a whole terrible history. He tells it what to do. He says where it came from ("from the howling of a poisonous flower"), he describes its physical appearance, he says what's inside it, he tells what it does, and he compares it to other things ("like the sun bleding from its claw / onto the sidewalk of clouds"). He also brings in some associations with other words, *sun* and *night*. He could have written entire poems—and quite different ones—for those words, too.

137

Have your students each think of a single strong word that for them has a powerful resonance, an emotional undertow. The word need not call up negative feelings. It might be the student's own name. It might be a spiritual word, such as *heaven* or *buddhahood*. It might be a word whose meaning the student doesn't know, but recalls for some mysterious reason. It might be a foreign word. It might be a long word, like *Mississippi*. Any word will do, so long as it has a fascination for the student. It's helpful to give the students some examples of your own and ask them for their suggestions. The crux of this assignment is the word chosen: it must have an emotional vibrancy for the writer, or else the resulting poem will be forced or flat. Don't be surprised if some of the words are scatalogical.

After each of the students has thought of a word, ask them to close their eyes and say it softly to themselves, or to hear it in their minds. Tell them to let their minds go with that word, to imagine where the word was born, what shape it might take if it were a person, animal, or object, what it would look like. Remind them that they can talk to the word, give it commands, or perhaps even have a conversation with it. Point out that, like Césaire, they might not want to disclose the word right away. The main thing for you is to create an atmosphere in which free association can thrive. As in Césaire's poem, free verse is probably the best vehicle for this assignment.

Césaire's *Collected Poems* runs to 424 large pages, from any of which you will find dazzling passages that unfortunately don't suggest a writing assignment. However, there is one assignment or procedure that you could use for any passage. As poet-teachers Julie Patton and Janice Lowe descibe in their essays elsewhere in this volume, you could read aloud to your students as they write, asking them to listen to you only when they've run out of words themselves, to take off from a phrase or an image that happens to be resonating in the air at that moment. There is no need for the student to "understand" the phrase or image, only to use it as a springboard to get back into the flow of their own poems. Césaire's poetry, so replete with energy and things and spirit, can be a marvelous catalyst.

Bibliography

Césaire, Aimé. *The Collected Poetry*. Translated by Clayton Eshleman and Annette Smith. Berkeley: University of California Press, 1983. This large volume, excellently translated, introduced, and annotated, is the mother lode of Césaire's poetry.

Kennedy, Ellen Conroy, ed. *The Negritude Poets: An Anthology of Translations from the French*. New York: Thunder's Mouth Press, 1989. This volume, which originally appeared in 1975, could use some minor updating, but it is still the single best introduction to the Negritude poets, with a wide selection, good introduction, excellent biographical notes on each poet, and a comprehensive bibliography. The book clarifies the links between the poets of the Harlem Renaissance, the Caribbean, Africa, and the Indian Ocean.

PEGGY GARRISON

Two Strings,
One Pierced Cry

Writing Poems from Two Points of
View Using Rita Dove's Poetry

MULTIPLE PERSPECTIVE is a prominent theme in Rita Dove's poetry. In her collection about her grandparents, *Thomas and Beulah,* the poems "Courtship" and "Courtship, Diligence" present the same situation, but each is told from a different point of view. Thomas has come to court Beulah, yet although they're both seated in the same parlor, their feelings and perceptions are not at all similar. In presenting these two characters' intimate viewpoints, Rita Dove gives the reader an expanded sense of honesty. She implies that if one set of emotional truths offers insight, then two sets can offer even greater insight.

The multiplicity of truth is an important artistic concept, and writing poems from two points of view is one effective way of introducing students to it. The following assignment can be used with students from fifth grade to college; I've used it both in a creative writing workshop at New York University and in a poetry residency at a combined elementary and middle school in Brooklyn. Though at first I felt this assignment probably wouldn't work below junior high school, my fifth grade "experiment" with it surprised both me and the classroom teacher.

For the college and eighth grade classes I began by handing out copies of the following two poems, which I asked a student to read aloud:

Courtship

1.
Fine evening may I have
the pleasure . . .
up and down the block
waiting—for what? A

magnolia breeze, someone
to trot out the stars?

But she won't set a foot
in his turtledove Nash,
it wasn't proper.
Her pleated skirt fans
softly, a circlet of arrows.

King of the Crawfish
in his yellow scarf,
mandolin belly pressed tight
to his hounds-tooth vest—
his wrist flicks for the pleats
all in a row, sighing . . .

2.
. . . so he wraps the yellow silk
still warm from his throat
around her shoulders. (He made
good money; he could buy another.)
A gnat flies
in his eye and she thinks
he's crying.

Then the parlor festooned
like a ship and Thomas
twirling his hat in his hands
wondering how did I get here.
China pugs guarding a fringed settee
where a father, half-Cherokee,
smokes and frowns.
I'll give her a good life—
what was he doing,
selling all for a song?
His heart fluttering shut
then slowly opening.

Courtship, Diligence

A yellow scarf runs through his fingers
as if it were melting.
Thomas dabbing his brow.

And now his mandolin in a hurry
though the night, as they say,
is young,
though she is *getting on.*

Hush, the strings tinkle. *Pretty gal.*

Cigar-box music!
She'd much prefer a pianola
and scent in a sky-colored flask.

Not that scarf, bright as butter.
Not his hands, cool as dimes.

Rita Dove's textured and complex imagery makes demands on the reader. When I discovered that some of my more literal-minded students found these poems somewhat baffling, I asked the following questions to help them to a clearer understanding:

1. These poems probably take place in the United States in the 1920s. How are "courting" customs different today?

2. What words are the same in both poems?

3. How do Thomas and Beulah differ in their perceptions of the scarf? Of the music?

4. How does Thomas think Beulah views the gnat?

5. Poetry often uses imagistic language. What is "scent in a sky-colored flask?" What are "China pugs guarding a fringed settee"?

6. Who do you think loves whom more? What kind of man would Beulah have preferred? Give evidence from the poem that focuses on her.

7. What does the word *diligence* mean, and how might it apply to Beulah?

8. What do you think the father's point of view might be?

After discussing these questions, I asked the students to write their own poems from two points of view. Together we shared some suggestions—parents vs. children, attitudes about snow, two "takes" on the same person—but I didn't want to define the exercise too rigidly. I wanted to leave enough room for the students to follow their own interpretations.

One adult student wrote about a wife and her husband beside a pool on a summer day:

The Pool

> The Wife
> It's egg-frying, branding-iron hot today
> Why should I care?
> I'm down at the pool
> About to charge full speed
> Into the cool, deep water,
> Arms extended, kick at the ready,
> Body and mind smooth and calm
> All things possible.

> Her Husband
> I'll just sit here by the edge
> and dangle my feet slowly.
> No need to go into the pool just yet.
> It's probably too cold.
> Swimming comes easy
> But it isn't fun.
> All those years I practiced kicking and stroking
> At the private school
> Have punctured pleasure.
> It really *is* too cold.
> Maybe tomorrow.

—*Joan Freeman*

Another described two people skiing down the same slope:

Double Diamond

Sleep.
Hop and turn, hop and turn.
I find that G-spot
    harmony of powder and exertion:
A frightening, thrilling release from gravity
before
    the next turn and safety, then off again.
It's the closest to flying dreams
In a white haze,
    no differentiation between earth and sky.
Suddenly the sun breaks through the overhead
veil,
    seeming to spotlight my glorious suspension,

A yellow bird with
    flakes sparkling round;
      carve into a stop.
Heart pounding, vision keeping time,
I fall over laughing, gasping, to wait for him.

      *

Skis peek out over the cornice.
Why here?
Heart pounds; altitude, fear.
I scan a route, pick a turn.
Miss.
Too much speed, hang on, hang on—turn!
Tips cross in the air;
      quickly unweight the upper.
My balance is all wrong.
flat light, camouflaging
      far from flat underneath.
A minefield.
I manage three, four turns;
      nearly halfway down,
Certainly like no hero
      in this descent to safety.
There, a clod of thickness lurking; right
      legs dig in, abruptly stop.
I lurch on and up around the pinned part,
forming some ghastly, overaged corkscrew.
I push on poles to extricate myself, but the
bottomless
      white gives no purchase.
Trapped and awkward, I pause to see a yellow
speck
      below wave at me.

    —Rebecca Leer

Maggie Kim's poem explored two different perceptions of the same
fashion model:

Bones. I look at her and all I see are the cheekbones, jarring
the lines of her face, the ribs barely caged by the
thin skin of her torso, the elbows and hips jutting like
defiant projectiles—daring anyone to get too close.

When she walks, she floats, practically airborne, certainly
weightless. She could fly away on a light breath; she would
crumble from a gentle shove.

Vacant eyes look back at me, oblivious.

     *

I dream of her sometimes when I look at her on my wall in a
magazine, on t.v. Beautifully fragile, her face and body
like a child's, a doll's: I think I could take care of her.

I'd dress her and she'd float next to me, practically airborne,
weightlessly graceful. My hand encircling her arm,
she'd follow where I led.

Looking into the depths of her eyes, I see an answer, that
she's the answer.

    —Maggie Kim

The eighth graders' poems often centered on conflicts with siblings
or parents:

I like this weather.
The sun is shining.
It's warm.
We are going to play outside.
Tomorrow we go to watch the basketball game.
My brother doesn't like this.

I hate the warm weather.
I'd rather sit here and watch cartoons.
I don't want to go to the basketball game.
I would go to play football.
I hate my brother who likes all this.

    —Umar Ali Faroogi

Parental Playground

My wife and I
We ride the swings of adolescence with her.
We balance the see-saw of truth and lies
for her.
We climb the monkey bars of heartache

with her.
When she falls off the swing
We help her up.

When she's stuck on the monkey bars
we help her,
and when she falls off the see-saw
we help her get back on.

Corporate Cry
(the teenager)

They don't know,
nobody knows
the torment of the word "no"—
the fierce sound of his roar
and how she manifestly shouts
No
No.
They think they're mending but
they're breaking.

    —Reyna Richman

I feared that the different-viewpoint concept would be over the fifth graders' heads and that the two sample poems would be too difficult for them, but their teacher suggested that I go ahead and try it, that often her students surprised even her.

I proceeded slowly, allowing two class periods rather than one to complete the assignment. We spent a lot of time discussing the two poems. Students found the idea of formal courting very different from today's more relaxed attitudes about dating. The words *mandolin*, *pianola*, *pugs*, and *festooned* needed to be defined, and of course nobody knew what a Nash was. (I sighed, picturing my little green Nash Rambler beside the yellowing elms in my college's parking lot thirty-five years ago.)

However, their insights into the characters of Thomas and Beulah were penetrating. One student said she felt sad for Thomas because he gave Beulah his scarf and played music for her and she didn't appreciate it. Another said Thomas loved Beulah more because he was more nervous than she. Another said Beulah was a hard person to satisfy. Although understanding the poems required effort, the students remained interested and focused throughout the discussion. They seemed proud to be successfully tackling difficult material.

As the following examples show, not only did the fifth graders grasp the double-viewpoint concept, they selected a variety of topics and handled them in original ways.

The Bahamas

I think the Bahamas are
a perfect vacation.
It's nice and warm
and you can always get a perfect tan.
The water is cool to swim in and
you can see everything underwater
because the water is clear.

I hate the Bahamas.
It's too hot and I definitely
would get a sunburn.
The water is way too warm and I
don't like anybody seeing how I swim.

—*Esada Nikocevic*

The Bungee Jump

A married couple are going bungee jumping.

Tom thinks:

This is going to be fun.
I'm going to tell all my friends.
Meg is going to love it also.
It's going to be the best.

Meg thinks:

This is suicide.
Is he crazy?
Oh my God, this is 1000 feet down.
Uh! I want a divorce.
I don't want to kill myself.
I'm getting out of here.

—*Dina Shenker*

Video Games

Fun and action packed,
long and hard.
Controls and a joystick = improved control and speed of my fingers,
tons of attacks and codes to learn = improves my memory.

Video Games: Dad's Side

Complete crap,
dull and waste of time.
Adam likes it; I have better things to do.
Mortgages and real estate's my job.
I spend long hours with my job.

—*Adam L. Hernandez*

The Cat

Me and my friend were walking and we saw a cat. I said, "I hate cats. They
might have a disease in their fur and I don't like their claws. They are too
sharp. They might scratch me."

Amy my friend said, "I love cats. They are so cute." And then she even
picked up the kitty cat and hugged it. She said, "Oh look at this brown fur
and those whiskers." And she said she was going to take it home and keep
it as a pet.

—*Karen Yip*

One woman said, "I'll definitely win this competition.
I'll rope climb faster than you. You're quite a
slow poke."

"I don't care who wins this race," said the
other. "Anyway, let's begin."

And so the race was begun,
and guess who won?
The other woman.

—*Ilona Ochertyanskaya*

I think the intimate tone of Rita Dove's two poems helped students handle the assignment in ways that were individual. Rather than choosing politically clichéd subjects, they wrote about personal material and were able to empathize convincingly with the different viewpoints of their characters. In addition, I would hope, they began to see how the pen (or the computer) might help them to examine and live with conflicts.

Bibliography

Bellin, Steven, "A Conversation with Rita Dove," *Mississippi Review,* Vol. 23, No. 3 (1995).

Dove, Rita, *Selected Poems.* New York: Vintage, 1993.

McDowell, Robert, "The Assembling Vision of Rita Dove," *Callaloo* 9 (Winter, 1986).

Rampersad, Arnold, "The Poems of Rita Dove," *Callaloo* 9 (Winter 1986).

Rubin, Stan Sanvel, and Earl G. Ingersoll, "A Conversation with Rita Dove," *Black American Literature Forum* 20 (Fall 1986).

Stein, Kevin, "Lives in Motion: Multiple Perspectives in Rita Dove's Poetry," *Mississippi Review,* Vol. 23, No. 3 (1995).

CATHERINE BARNETT

Square Toes and Icy Arms

How to Simplify As You Personify

"IS ANGER A MAN or a woman?" I asked a student in class last week. The young woman—she is sixteen and has a one-year-old son—thought for a long moment, about to give up. "Tell me what Anger looks like," I asked, "where he or she lives. Close your eyes and tell me everything you know about this character." I roamed around the classroom, and when I made it back to her desk, she had written:

> Anger's hands are hammers. His teeth are two-edged swords. His head is made of stone. Anger has no face, just two beady little eyes. His eyebrows always hang low. Anger tastes bitter.

This exchange took place during one of my favorite exercises. The student's writing owes its energy and power to passages from Zora Neale Hurston's autobiography, *Dust Tracks on a Road*, and her novel, *Their Eyes Were Watching God*. Throughout these works, Hurston personifies both the fictional and real worlds, turning philosophical concepts (like time and fate), life passages (like death), and even the weather into active characters.

In *Their Eyes*, she uses an unusual personification to describe the damage wrought by a flood: "Havoc was there with her mouth wide open." The overflowing lake itself takes on human characteristics: thunder "woke up old Okechobee and the monster began to roll in his bed. Began to roll and complain like a peevish world on a grumble. . . . The people felt uncomfortable but safe because there were the seawalls to chain the senseless monster in his bed." Hurston gives the sun a distinct personality throughout the novel. Janie, the main character, goes to bed one night filled with doubt about her new husband, Tea-Cake, who had disappeared with her money. It is the sun who first reassures her:

> Janie dozed off to sleep but she woke up in time to see the sun sending up spies ahead of him to mark out the road through the dark. He peeped

up over the door sill of the world and made a little foolishness with red. But pretty soon, he laid all that aside and went about his business dressed all in white.

Night, too, takes on human characteristics in Hurston's Florida: "Night was striding across nothingness with the whole round world in his hands."

In *Dust Tracks on a Road*, Hurston writes that "fate was watching us and laughing" and that Hurston herself has "been in Sorrow's kitchen and licked out all the pots." In an unpublished chapter, Hurston personifies Time, calling him "hungry" as he "squats" and "waits." She sees his footprints, and gazes into his reflections:

> His frame was made out of emptiness, and his mouth set wide for prey. Mystery is his oldest son, and power is his portion. For it was said on the day of first sayings that Time should speak backward over his shoulder, and none should see his face. . . .

Death makes a dramatic appearance in both Hurston's novel and in her autobiography. In *Their Eyes*, Janie encounters Death as she watches her husband grow weak:

> So Janie began to think of Death. Death, that strange being with the huge square toes who lived way in the West. The great one who lived in a straight house like a platform without sides to it, and without a roof. What need has Death for a cover, and what winds can blow against him? He stands in his high house that overlooks the world. Stands watchful and motionless all day with his sword drawn back, waiting for the messenger to bid him come. Been standing there before there was a where or a when or a then. She was liable to find a feather from his wings lying in her yard any day now. . . .

In a deft 100 words, Hurston manages to give the idea of death a home, gestures, a history, feathers, and flesh.

Those eerie square toes reappear in her autobiography as she describes the day her mother died. Hurston was nine years old and no match against "that two-headed spirit that rules the beginning and end of things called Death."

> The Master-Maker in His making had made Old Death. Made him with big, soft feet and square toes. Made him with a face that reflects the face of all things, but neither changes itself, nor is mirrored anywhere. Made the body of Death out of infinite hunger. Made a weapon for his hand to

satisfy his needs. . . . Death had no home and he knew it at once. . . . He was already old when he was made. . . . Death finished his prowling through the house on his padded feet and entered the room. He bowed to Mama. . . .

Try reading either of these passages aloud—several times over—to a class of students and see how the room quiets. I've read Hurston's work to fourth, fifth, and sixth graders, and to a group of teen mothers. Something about those square toes and that feather—you can see it sailing slowly to the inevitable ground—stops chatter and commands attention.

I like to give the students examples of personification from other writers, if time allows. A poem titled "Go Down Death" by James Weldon Johnson (who with his brother composed "Lift Every Voice and Sing," a song once known as the Negro national anthem) complements Hurston's prose. Death appears in the third stanza of Johnson's poem:

And that tall, bright angel cried in a voice
That broke like a clap of thunder:
Call Death!—Call Death!
And the echo sounded down the streets of heaven
Till it reached away back to that shadowy place,
Where Death waits with his pale, white horses.

And Death heard the summons,
And he leaped on his fastest horse,
Pale as a sheet in the moonlight.
Up the golden street Death galloped,
And the hoof of his horse struck fire from the gold,
But they didn't make no sound. . . .

Later in the poem, Johnson writes that Death "didn't say a word, / But he loosed the reins on his pale, white horse / And he clamped the spurs to his bloodless sides. . . . And the foam from his horse was like a comet in the sky." At the end of this poem, Death cradles a smiling woman in his "icy arms."

The contrasts between Hurston's and Johnson's personfications help students realize that there is no "right" way to treat something that is as universal as death. And the simple fact that both writers end up with such peculiar and striking images—that Death can take such different guises, unique to each writer's vision—leads the class naturally to an all-important discussion of clichés and how to avoid them.

The best way to get around clichés, I tell students (and myself), is to be as specific as possible. Two fifth graders' efforts with this exercise provide good examples of how to dig beneath the surface of clichés. One girl began with a stereotype, defining "courage" rather than personifying it. "Courage," she wrote, "is a brave person who is not afraid of anything." But as she worked she began to discover more about her character:

> Courage is a man of human size. He wears a white t-shirt and tight blue jeans and has a beautiful voice. He is nineteen years old. He's 100 times stronger than any man. He can lift up the Empire State Building.

Imagining herself as Courage, another girl worked her way from the general—"I am invisible"—to the very specific:

> I can only be seen in the dark. I sneak in people's houses when they are afraid. I calm them down by putting their hands on my heart. . . . I like to drink rain and eat five feet of clouds a day for breakfast, lunch, and dinner. I sleep underground where the ants live.

Along with my plea—this prayer! this push!—for specificity and detail comes another, equally essential to this (and every) exercise: *include the five senses.* Johnson's poem illustrates the power of sensory detail: his Death has those "icy arms," his horse is silent as it gallops down the gold street.

By now some students may be getting confused. Two Deaths, five senses, a dozen details—what's going on? If so, a brief discussion of personification is in order. "How and why give human traits to something as seemingly abstract as death?" I ask them. I encourage the students to name some other abstractions they might want to personify.

I often make this same mistake: at the mention of "abstract," faces go blank, so I simply ask the students for words they hear over and over—words they've heard so often they've lost their meaning. Words like death, love, happiness. What others? As a class, we create a list. Even though these words are universal, the lists reflect the make-up and concerns of each class. At a school in uptown Manhattan, for example, fifth graders thought of Trouble, Fear, Racism, Greed, and Courage. A class of teen mothers came up with Depression, Fatigue, and Ambition.

It is often a good idea to start by writing a group description. This loosens everybody up, and creates a mood for writing. The students choose which word they want to transform into a character; a group of teen mothers, for example, chose "Pain." I usually ask a few leading questions, borrowing heavily from Hurston and Johnson and encouraging students to bring the senses into their descriptions. With the teen mothers, responses came fast. "Pain," they said (as I wrote their words on the blackboard),

> . . . wears dirty sneakers and a black sweatshirt. He lives on the corner of your block, an unwanted visitor. He has gold teeth, an afro, dirty fingernails. He never uses condoms. His voice is rusty, scratchy, screechy. He says, "I love you, I love you, I love you. Hi Baby. Suffer. You look good." He tastes like lime and hot sweat. His face feels like alligator skin. He has calluses all over his feet. He's afraid of losing honor.

Soon I ask each student to choose his or her own word from the long list of words on the board and to create a living, breathing character out of it.

"You never hear Fatigue," wrote one fifteen-year-old mother who had given birth six weeks earlier. "He is so quiet and smooth. He comes to you like thirst and leaves like wind. He touches the weakest part of your body, which is your eyes. He lives anywhere he wants to live. . . ." Her friend, also the mother of a young boy, discovered a very different Fatigue:

> Fatigue drags her feet all day. Her shoes make a scraping sound against the ground and whenever she passes by someone they yawn. She carries a pillow and blanket in a shopping cart, along with a clown. When she pulls the clown's chord it plays "Rock-A-Bye Baby" and that soothes her. . . . Her voice is gentle and she is soft spoken. Her mellow voice will hypnotize you and make you sleepy. She always says Relax, don't work so hard, there's always tomorrow. . . .

Another young mother wrote a brief sketch of Ambition, a woman who "walks with her head high":

> She wears yellow. When you look at her she slows and dazzles in front of your eyes. Her hair and nails are always neatly done. . . . She carries a crystal rock in her pocket. She always says believe in yourself and you can do anything.

A fourth grader with learning disabilities described Fear as someone who "brings a warrant made out of fire." Peace, wrote one of his classmates, "is a lady with love written all over her." Love is always a popular figure in this exercise, and appears in many guises. One defiant fifth grade boy surprised his classmates with his portrait of Love as a man who carries a suitcase. He smells like apples. He wears black pants, a white t-shirt, white shiny shoes. . . . In his suitcase he carries presents for his wife and love poems. He has friends who say, "We care about you." He gives everyone presents and sometimes says I love you. Every day he goes to church and prays.

Two third grade girls came up with very different pictures of Love. "Love is when the sky turns blue," wrote one shy girl. "She comes knocking on my door quietly. Then she calls my name five times. And I say, "Who is it? Who is it? Who is it?" Her classmate saw Love as a boy. "When I hug him," she wrote, "it feels like his eye has heaven in it." At a neighboring desk, a boy wrote about "Anger, a man with a black robe":

> His eyes are strange. One of them is black and one of them is brown. When he touches the ground it cracks. He goes down into the ground and says, "Come, Michael, Come." And I follow him to the underground. I see angry faces. I was saying, "It can't be true. It can't be true. It can't be true." And everything in the underground faded and he said, "Please don't leave me. Please, Please."

Happiness, wrote another third grader, "looks like my grandmother. She is wearing black pants and a black shirt. She is carrying presents. She lights candles."

After reading aloud the Hurston or Johnson excerpt (or both), you might choose a few of he following personification sketches by third, fourth, and fifth grade students to demonstrate how others have transformed words like Wealth, Jealousy, and Sadness into characters of their own.

> Wealth is somebody who is dressed in a polka-dot suit. I call him when me and my sister need some cash in our stash. When he comes to give us money he drops a gold coin on the ground. And then he throws a sack of money to each of us. His teeth are yellow and his face is green and his eyes are blue, and his ears are flat but oval shaped. All the time in his pockets he has gold coins. Real gold coins. And he never spends his money. He saves it up all the time.

Jealousy goes around looking at things that other people have that he wants. He is always jealous of the clothes they wear, the things they carry out. He mumbles to himself, "I wish I had that," with a frown on his face. I always see him at the bakery buying a muffin. When he sees me he says, "Get out of my way, kid, you bother me!" I don't know what he has in his suitcase, but people say he carries a dead bird in there. I think he keeps it for good luck.

Sadness has sad, big, blue eyes and skinny lips. He smells like the breeze in the sun. He has a deep low voice. He is never happy and he carries a broken heart in his hand. You can see him in the alleys at night. He is very skinny and has little toes. He wears only a worn-out suit.

Joy looks like an elf. He wears a green overcoat and green tight pants. He carries many, many presents. His voice is very high and screechy. He has white hair and a long beard. You can find him on special occasions.

Sadness just came to my house. All she did was ask for sugar, but she looked so sad her eyes were watery. . . . She told me her daughter just died. She got hit by a car. And she could remember when she held her in her arms when she was born. The old lady has bags on her eyes. She has a cane. She was leaning on me crying.

This exercise acquaints students with Hurston's work and with the technique of personification, and it can also lead them to their best writing. The pleasure of reading Hurston's prose aloud is soon matched by listening to the students read their own. Their images are often so strong that their descriptions—like Hurston's—approach the intensity and lyricism of prose poems.

Bibliography

(*Note: All Hurston quotations are from the two books noted below; the James Weldon Johnson poem "Go Down Death" appears in many anthologies; I found it in* American Negro Poetry, *edited by Arna Bontemps.*)

Bontemps, Arna, ed. *American Negro Poetry*. New York: HarperCollins, 1996.

Hurston, Zora Neale. *Dust Tracks on a Road: An Autobiography*. New York: HarperCollins, 1991.

———. *Their Eyes Were Watching God*. New York, Harper & Row, 1990.

PATRICIA SPEARS JONES

Experience, Experiment

Using Black Poetry in Creative Writing Classes

Introduction

It is surprising that few writing teachers seem to use work from the African American branch of the American literary canon. Or when they do, they rely on familiar poets such as Langston Hughes and Gwendolyn Brooks or on works based on popular culture, such as rap. They remain less than willing to familiarize themselves with the astonishing range of work that could well serve poetry students from beginners to advanced students of this great art. Just to give a writing instructor an idea of that range, one could work with the narrative and persona poems by Ai and Rita Dove, the linguistic investigations of Lorenzo Thomas and Nathaniel Mackey, and the blues-based work of Sterling Brown or spoken-word veteran Sekou Sundiata.

The Usual Suspect: Gwendolyn Brooks

A few years ago I taught a community workshop entitled "Approaches to Writing History in Poetry." My aim was to get the participants to use narrative and their own personal take on historical events. One of the poets whose work served to spark discussion and inspire students was Gwendolyn Brooks. I used her poem, "The Chicago Defender Sends a Man to Little Rock." An excellent introduction to Brooks's formal strategies and recurrent themes, this poem also gets students to look more carefully at ways to use formal techniques. In delving into the psychological and professional turmoil faced by the poem's speaker, Ms. Brooks uses elements found in her best work: well-executed rhyme scheme, unabashed Christian symbolism, and irony to undercut flourishes of sentimentality. The poem's narrator couches his outrage at the treatment of The Little Rock Nine, the Black students who integrated Central High School in 1957. In this poem, Brooks covers more ground than in the often used "We Real Cool." "The Chicago Defender" inspires students to explore an array of methods to convey a speaker's voice and the complicated relationship of narrator to subject. In the penultimate stanza, the poet's control is well displayed:

> And true, they are hurling spittle, rock,
> Garbage and fruit in Little Rock.
> And I saw coiling storm a-writhe
> On bright madonnas. And a scythe
> Of men harrassing brownish girls.
> (The bows and barrettes in the curls
> And braids declined away from joy.)
> I saw a bleeding brownish boy. . . .

Gwendolyn Brooks uses formal poetic techniques in the service of difficult, occasionally radical ideas, thus providing quite a different model from many others who use the same techniques.

Point of View and Narrative: Ai

In collections with titles such as *Cruelty, Sin, Fate,* and *Greed,* Ai investigates the moral, historical, and spiritual crises of our times. Ai's work liberates writers from the prison that identity politics can become. Creating a persona, analyzing popular mythologies, and messing with historical fact to get to a greater emotional truth are Ai's gifts to contemporary poetics. And she does it with that most Victorian of vehicles, the dramatic monologue. An excellent example is her poem, "Knockout," told in the voice of a drug-addicted prostitute. This poem, which frames the Mike Tyson rape case in a poor and extremely vulnerable woman's voice, uses a raw, artful street language to highlight our society's ambivalence towards rape in the black community and the woman's condemnation of misogyny and class bias in society in general.

Persona poems are extremely useful for exploring the psychological in poetry. In developing persona, writers have to find "otherness" and empathy for characters real or imagined. Persona provides the perfect opportunity to experiment with levels of diction and helps students see how difference is evoked through language. It also allows writers the opportunity to explore challenging ideas and issues (ethnic identity, family difficulties, historical misdeeds) by distancing the writer from the poem's speaker—a historical figure, a distant relative (such as a grandparent or uncle from the "Old Country"), or the prostitute in

Ai's "Knockout." This strategy can provide students with a greater insight into the human condition by having them get inside of characters that are only seemingly alien from their own.

Of course the sexual explicitness of some of Ai's poems make them suitable only for certain audiences. Use your good judgement.

Folklore, Folklife and All That Jazz: Sterling Brown and Ishmael Reed

All too often in school, ethnic dialect, mythology, and folklore are narrowly conceptualized and rarely connected to contemporary concerns. However, the folkloric can provide rich possibilities for today's students. Two poets who present contrasting aspects of this kind of work are Sterling Brown, whose *Southern Road* is a classic volume of Southern idioms, and Ishmael Reed, for whom the folkloric is clearly global in character. Brown and Reed use tales of tricksters and blues-based suites of words to convey the astonishing survival skills of African Americans.

In Brown's Slim Geer series, Slim Geer is the hero of many a tall tale, like Paul Bunyan or John Henry, but his is the story of the trickster, the hipster, the con man staying alive during the Jim Crow era. While Brown's work covers some of the same ground as Langston Hughes's, Brown's poems stay closer to the narrative of folktales, the rural equivalent of Hughes's urban ones. The poems in *Southern Road* achieve the haunting quality of a series of ghost stories.

The power of Brown's poems comes from his capacity to make ballads filtered through a blues sensibility. He uses dialect and well-selected details that further the poem's narrative, and he introduces irony, rage, and the occasional dark laughter, as in "Kentucky Blues," whose hard-luck narrator declares:

> Cornland good,
> Tobacco land fine,
> Can't raise nothin'
> On dis hill o' mine
> [. . .]
> De red licker's good
> An' it ain't too high,
> Gonna brag about Kentucky
> Till I die. . . .

The ballad can be an excellent starting point for poets with limited skills because its structure allows for narrative and invention while adhering to a set pattern. Use of folklore and folklife could provide students with appropriate subject matter and a way to integrate their own lives and the stuff of legends.

While Sterling Brown's work incorporates American blues still close to its rural roots, Ishmael Reed presents a more urban and urbane strain of the blues sensibility. Reed's work is founded on his knowledge of African American culture and on a knowledge of myth, ritual, history, and psychology that is transatlantic. Clearly a disciple of Brown, Reed incorporates the word play associated with the blues but with a modernist twist. In the "The Reactionary Poet"—in which he displays his talent for being the great contrarian of African American letters—he creates a terrific list based on early twentieth-century popular culture, such as: "Bring back suspenders! / . . . Picnics in the park / Flagpole sitting / Straw hats / Rent parties / Corn liquor / The banjo / Georgia quilts / Krazy Kat / Restock / The syncopation of / Fletcher Henderson / The Kiplingesque lines / of James Weldon Johnson. . . ." Reed's list creates a sense of the "colored" 1920s, a counter-narrative to the Lost Generation of Hemingway, Dorothy Parker, and T. S. Eliot.

An excellent assignment for more advanced writers is to create ballads that flow from these two radically different voicings of the American experience as seen through the blues sensibility. Using twentieth-century slang, modernist concepts, and contrasting structures (ballad versus collage) provides an exciting challenge poets at any stage in their development.

Experience, Experiment: Lorenzo Thomas

If there is a common ground for African American poets, it is reflection, signification, and rage in response to the racism, hypocrisy, violence—"the high cost of living" as Angela Jackson has called it—faced by African Americans. Given these concerns, Black culture is sometimes seen from the outside as homogenous, even though African Americans are as diverse as any other group in America, a country that is partly defined by its African American roots. The irony of this cultural and occasional linguistic double bind—some call it Ebonics—is artfully captured in the experimental work of poets such as Lorenzo Thomas.

For the student of contemporary American poetics, Thomas models great poetic behavior. His work is influenced by the formal structures favored by Brooks and poets of her generation; the folkloric aspects of African American culture, especially the blues quatrain of Brown; by the narrative strategies that Ai focuses on, as well as Reed's ironic response to cross-cultural issues and his creation of counter-narratives to official history. But Thomas has developed a unique voice over the past thirty years, one that engages and inspires writing students unafraid of form and content that are challenging.

In poems such as "My Office" and "They Never Lose," Thomas explores the trickster ways—part hipster, part hippie, always black—as his narrators observe cultural permutations, disruptions, and displacements. Any poet who can write lines such as "you want an apple or a wedding ring? / Paris my foot. The thought! That stuck-up / Sucker / One man, three women / Who he think he is?" from "They Never Loose" is a poet in touch with his own soul's power to withstand the daily absurdity that is modern life.

In many ways Thomas shares his ironic yet spiritual sense of daily struggle with James Schuyler. There is an offhandedness in Thomas's work that either confuses or beguiles students. What is at work is the risk in language, its obliqueness as well as its transparency. Sophisticated students of contemporary literature would do well to look at the way Thomas uses both popular culture and "high art" content, such as nineteenth-century European painting and ancient and modern African religions. And yet, like Frank O'Hara, Thomas has the ability to shift tone as quickly as he turns the corner from Fifth Avenue to Spanish Harlem.

Conclusion

The imaginative teacher of writing has a wide range of African American perspectives to share with students. The poets considered here offer students an opportunity to refresh and expand their concepts of writing and to respond to language in a new way. Poetry offers special opportunities for linguistic invention and the discovery of emotional truths. Gwendolyn Brooks, Ai, Sterling Brown, Ishmael Reed, and Lorenzo Thomas are a few of the African Americans writing in the twentieth century who have made and are making this exciting and sometimes perilous journey.

Bibliography

Ai. *Greed*. New York: Norton, 1993.

Brooks, Gwendolyn. *Blacks*. Chicago: Third World Press, 1991.

Brown, Sterling. *Southern Road*. Boston: Beacon, 1932.

Reed, Ishmael. *New and Collected Poems*. New York: Atheneum, 1988.

Thomas, Lorenzo. *Chances Are Few*. Berkeley: Blue Wind, 1979.

MARGOT FORTUNATO GALT

The Great Migration

Using the Art of Jacob Lawrence and the Poetry of Langston Hughes and Gwendolyn Brooks

IN 1996, the artist Jacob Lawrence had a show at the University of Minnesota's Weisman Art Gallery, which I saw with a fourth grade class from St. Paul's Mississippi Arts Magnet Elementary School, where I was writer-in-residence.

Beforehand, I had read an interview with Lawrence and his wife, which was accompanied by reproductions of his boldly colored work, angular and full of movement. I was especially intrigued by his early series of paintings called *The Migration Series*. Lawrence was born in 1917 in New Jersey, the son of two African Americans traveling north from Virginia and South Carolina, spurred by poverty and prejudice in the South, lured by jobs created by World War I in the North. The family met others on their way to Pittsburgh, New York, Chicago, Detroit, Cleveland, and St. Louis. Eventually, his family also continued north, settling in Harlem when Lawrence was thirteen. As he wrote, "Harlem was crowded with newcomers. . . . I grew up knowing about people on the move from the time I could understand what words meant."[1]

The students at Mississippi Magnet would know in their own way what he meant: Asian Americans from Laos, Cambodia, Thailand, and Vietnam; African Americans, many from Chicago or Gary and before that, Mississippi or Alabama; Mexican Americans and Latinos; white students of various ethnic backgrounds; and a few Native Americans. Because it's an arts magnet school, attracting students from the entire city, the students are also from quite different socio-economic groups. Many have moved more than once within the United States, so virtually all the students have family stories of migration and immigration.

On the bus ride to the gleaming cubist castle of the Weisman Art Gallery, I chatted with an African American girl who had been too shy to write during my first three days in class. She wasn't shy today. I had high hopes that she and the rest of the class would be roused by Lawrence's bold, graphic style. I also kept my fingers crossed that I'd find a way to bring the images from the show into the classroom, and that inspiration would help me link the story of the Great Migration to poetry.

At the museum, docents took small groups of students around, and I flitted from group to group. I learned about Lawrence's series honoring Toussaint L'Ouverture, the leader of revolt in Haiti; I saw more recent work in homage to Civil Rights leaders and events. Then, in the bookstore, I discovered *The Great Migration*, a beautiful book containing Lawrence's migration paintings, accompanied by his spare, eloquent text. I bought it and a box of notecards with images from the series, as well as other paintings by Lawrence in the same bold, angular style. The images on the notecards were melancholy, romantic, and political. Each card had a brief commentary on the back.[2]

Step One: Looking at Images and Talking about History

The next day in class, I read to the students from the Lawrence book, holding it up so they could see the illustrations. This second time through, we paused to examine the way Lawrence's images create meaning. We saw how he smoothes out individual faces, focusing instead on hats or clothing or body and posture. In a painting of a crowd pushing toward station exits for three destinations—Chicago, New York, and St. Louis—we feel the claustrophobic press of the faceless mass and imagine ourselves lost in the crowd, swept along by its momentum, the way blacks from the South must have felt moving to the North. In another painting, an outline of blackbirds above the heads of the travelers suggests the way we associate human migration with the migration of birds. One painting isolates a smokestack and bell on the train engine. The next picture shows sleeping forms in train seats.

Many pictures in *The Great Migration* show the extreme poverty of African Americans in the South. A couple with bowed heads sits before empty plates; a skinny child peers at the top of the table where a woman hacks at a narrow loaf; a single candle stands out against a wall. I told the students how the boll weevil ruined cotton crops for many years in the South, and how "race leaders" (the phrase of blacks at the time) like

George Washington Carver sought to introduce new farming practices and uses for other crops, such as peanuts.

Lawrence's paintings also portray the injustices of tenant farming and racism. In one, a huddled figure sits under a noose. This image gave me a chance to talk about lynching. In another, we see three figures, their backs to the viewer, heavy gold handcuffs linking them together, silhouetted against heavy bars. "Early arrival [at the station] was not easy, because African Americans found on the street could be arrested for no reason," the text explains. The painting juxtaposes the facelessness of these figures and the imposing power of the white legal system; the bright gold of the handcuffs adds a heavy irony.

By this point in the story, the motif that Lawrence repeats in the text—"And the migrants kept coming"—has established their courage and determination, and also the sense that the movement is bigger than any individual or obstacle. Describing factory labor agents who came South to recruit migrants and letters that arrived from friends already in the North, Lawrence builds up momentum toward the mid-point of the story: "Many migrants arrived in Chicago." Here the faces have more individuality: moustaches, different profiles, and always different hats. The first Northern images Lawrence creates are of industry and labor—pouring steel, a huge spike driven into a railroad. The refrain— "And the migrants kept coming"—now begins to suggest that the North accepted the migrants first as workers. Likewise, as Lawrence writes in the text, "Southern landowners, stripped of cheap labor, tried to stop the migration by jailing the labor agents and the migrants." The South considered the migrants mainly as laborers, too.

One painting shows migrants arriving in Pittsburgh: steep, unlit stairs with only a distant moon at the top; bars of many bedsteads crowded into one small room. Images of housing emphasize difficulties of the new life. Lawrence also uses harsh angles to depict the violence against the new migrants in the North—fists raised with clubs and knives, and flames destroying an apartment building. "Many northern workers were angry because they had to compete with the migrants for housing and jobs. There were riots."

Storefront churches and children at chalkboards suggest the benefits of the migration. Another painting shows parents who "gained the freedom to vote." "And the migrants kept coming." The final painting shows a crowd of travelers waiting beside a train track. Reds and yellows highlight hats or coats or suitcases against the pervasive dark greens and blacks of the rest of the figures. These vibrant colors connect with Lawrence's final passage: "Theirs is a story of African American strength and courage. I share it now as my parents told it to me, because their struggles and triumphs ring true today. People all over the world are still on the move, trying to build better lives for themselves and for their families." Thus, he brings the story into the present and connects it to young people with their own stories of change.

Step Two: Group Brainstorming and Ballad Writing

Although I didn't follow this step with the Mississippi Magnet School students, the next time I tried this exercise with a fifth grade class (at another school) we did some collaborative brainstorming before writing individual poems. I recommend this as a next step. I put the word MIGRATION on the chalkboard with lines radiating from it, as the beginning of a word map. Then I read to the students from Lawrence's book and asked them to note down phrases from the text and impressions of the paintings. Here is what these fifth graders came up with:

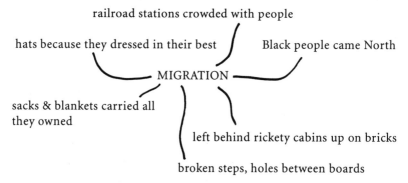

Next, I asked the students to talk about their own histories of immigration or migration. I recalled that racial discrimination extended even to transportation: in Charleston, South Carolina, where I grew up in the 1950s, blacks were allowed to ride only in the back of the bus. We then made another word map beside the first one, adding details of a Hmong family's escape through the jungles of Laos into Thailand, which the students had heard a few days before; a little about my Italian grandfather, who had immigrated from Italy in 1900 to New York, knowing no English; and a bit from a poem of mine.

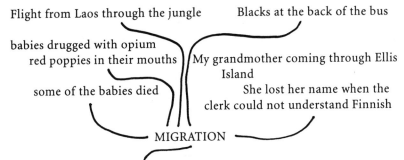

Flight from Laos through the jungle · Blacks at the back of the bus

babies drugged with opium
red poppies in their mouths · My grandmother coming through Ellis Island
She lost her name when the clerk could not understand Finnish

some of the babies died

MIGRATION

My grandfather sat on the steps of a church
A policeman asked him in English, he could only
answer Italian. Then surprise—the policeman spoke
Italian back, took him home for the night, and
put him on the train in the morning.

With the two word maps side by side, we talked about ways we could create a group poem using images from Lawrence's paintings and phrases from our own stories of migration. Noting that repeating the phrase "And the migrants kept coming" gave Lawrence's story a mythic, song-like quality and helped to unify the story, we decided to use the repeating phrase "railroad stations crowded with people," which we could alter slightly for different locations—e.g., "the banks of the Mekong river crowded with people" or "Ellis Island crowded with people."

I then suggested that the students do some oral history with their parents or other family members before the next class to broaden the range of stories that we had to draw on.

Each student then illustrated one moment in his or her family story and wrote a sentence or two to accompany the illustration.

That done, I had the students bring up their drawings to show and talk about. Then I selected one as a model, brainstormed a number of phrases of description and narrative about it, and wrote a verse of four lines or so, to combine with a repeating chorus.

Once students see how a verse is created—I pitch free verse, and compression and strong imagery—they are usually ready to write a verse or two of their own. They also see how the chorus or refrain can be altered to suggest different contexts. At this point the class composed a group poem and read it aloud, each writer reading his or her own section.

Step Three: Writing Individual Poems about Lawrence's Paintings, Using Poems by Langston Hughes and Gwendolyn Brooks as Inspiration

With the fourth graders who had seen Lawrence's work at the Weisman Gallery, I had already spent three days introducing them to free verse poetry and various brainstorming strategies. Thus, after reading *The Great Migration* to the class, we moved to individual poems. First we read several from Gwendolyn Brooks's first book, *A Street in Bronzeville*. Her poem "kitchenette building" suggests what happens to the dreams that recent migrants brought to Chicago:

> But could a dream send up through onion fumes
> Its white and violet, fight
> [. . .]
> Flutter, or sing an aria down these rooms. . . .

"The Bean Eaters," from a later collection by that name, shows what happens to an old couple who "eat beans mostly," but remember "with twinklings and twinges, / As they lean over the beans in their rented back room. . . ." Section I of the longer poem, "Bronzeville Woman in a Red Hat," depicts the racism that many migrants encountered when they took jobs in the homes of white Chicagoans, such as the black maid in this poem:

> They had never had one in the house before.
>   The strangeness of it all. Like unleashing
> A lion, really. Poised
> To pounce. A puma. A panther. A black
> Bear.
> There it stood in the door,
> Under a red hat that was rash, but refreshing—
> In a tasteless way, of course—across the dull dare,
> The semi-assault of that extraordinary blackness.
> The slackness
> Of that light pink mouth told little. The eyes told of heavy care. . . .
> But that was neither here nor there,
> And nothing to a wage-paying mistress as should
> Be getting her due whether life had been good
> For her slave, or bad.

There it stood
In the door. They had never had
One in the house before.

The students and I talked about how the poem's speaker uses animal images to describe the presence of the black woman in the doorway. We commented on both the wildness and power that the animals convey, and the fear we would feel if a puma or bear stood in our doorway. We then noticed how the poem's speaker proceeded to demolish that fear and make the black woman into a human with a hat. The kind of hat—tasteless—tells us that the speaker considers the woman inferior, and thus feels justified in her getting "her due," for the money she is paying, no matter whether this woman had had a hard life.

By the end of the poem, we understood that the "mistress" had reduced the black woman to "a slave," refusing to feel any concern for her as a human being. The stark contrast between the red hat and the woman's "extraordinary blackness" also reminded us of some of Lawrence's images in *The Great Migration*, where brightly colored, very individual hats rode on profiles that could belong to anyone. Gwendolyn Brooks's poem thus added an ironic interpretation to Lawrence's images by raising the idea that racism erases real, individual lives and puts stereotypes in their place.

This poem made a good connection to the next one I read the students, "Mother to Son" by Langston Hughes:

Well, son, I'll tell you:
Life for me ain't been no crystal stair.
It's had tacks in it,
And splinters,
And boards torn up,
And places with no carpet on the floor—
Bare.
But all the time
I'se been a-climbin' on,
And reachin' landin's,
And turnin' corners,
And sometimes goin' in the dark
Where there ain't been no light.
So boy, don't you turn back.
Don't you set down on the steps
'Cause you finds it's kinder hard.

Don't you fall now—
For I'se still goin', honey,
I'se still climbin',
And life for me ain't been no crystal stair.

This poem's powerful metaphor for city life, the wooden stairs of walk-up apartment buildings, resonates with many of Lawrence's dramatic images of the migration to—and life in—northern cities. I think particularly of his desolate wooden stairs with only a distant moon through a tall window lighting the way. The students and I talked about how both Lawrence and Hughes reduce their images to the most essential details. We also commented on the differences: how Lawrence's generic images portray an entire community, and Hughes focuses on the voice of one particular person speaking to another individual. I suggested that one strategy the students could use would be to bring to life a particular figure and give that person a voice that speaks for individual experience. They could do this whether or not there is actually a person in the painting; for instance, they could imagine someone outside the frame about to walk into the scene.

We also talked about the meaning of the crystal stair, juxtaposed with the wooden stairs, in the Hughes poem. The crystal stair seems to represent heavenly promises of a better life, the hopes that propelled African Americans out of the South. The wooden stairs, and the way the mother kept climbing no matter how hard the going, seems to resonate with the difficulties of those migrating North. The mother's phrase "I'se been climbin' on" echoes Lawrence's "And the migrants kept coming."

Step Four: Drafting Individual Poems

After this group discussion, I had the students choose images that they'd like to work with. Because I had only one copy of *The Great Migration*, I used the Jacob Lawrence notecards and a handful of postcards with images from the book. Thus students wrote about a variety of paintings, including *The Library, Community, Dreams,* and *Dancing Doll.* Spanning Lawrence's career from the 1940s to the 1970s, these paintings depict scenes from African American life and use the angular shapes, sharply constrasting tones, and unusual perspectives that

Lawrence developed in his migration series. A few sets of color xeroxes of the paintings would also have been helpful.

I gave the students a few final suggestions:

1. Notice how important the colors are in the paintings. Ask yourself where your eye goes first in the painting, and begin your poem with that detail. Then weave colors into as many lines as you can.

2. Don't write more than a few lines about any one detail.

3. Adopt a persona—that is, imagine you're speaking for someone in the painting or just beyond the frame.

4. Remember that your words have to stand for the image. Don't be afraid to say what seems obvious—for example, "three men—we see only their backs" or "the boy stands on tiptoe." The reader will "see" only what is written or suggested in words.

5. Capture the mood of the painting—activity, despair, hunger, determination, defeat, hope, dream, frustration, triumph, fear, etc.—by using images from the painting, and elaborate on them. The images themselves will carry the mood.

6. Shift between external description and interior states, such as wishes, hopes, dreams.

7. Remember, this is a poem. Don't be afraid to leap around a bit—in other words, you don't have to describe one corner of the painting, then another, and so on. You can let a color lead you in different directions within the painting, or let one tiny detail stand for a section of it—"gold handcuffs on their hands" might be all you'll say about the lower third of the painting.

The resulting poems were very satisfying, and in some cases dazzling. The girl who had been so shy on the bus to the exhibit raised her hand more than once to talk about her writing. She even read her draft aloud to the class.

Two of the best poems were about the same painting:

The Migration Problem

The big black iron bars with blue sky in between
Big strong backs facing me.
Hands hanging down, with cuffs around them.
The one in the middle wears a red shirt.
The first person, his head on his shoulders

There stand three men going to jail because
of a crime they didn't commit.
I'm in the middle seeing that I thought I was dumb
But really I wasn't, for I can't believe they'd lock
their own cousins up.

    —Jesse Docken, fourth grade

The hat and the coat matches on each person
Black bars beside the men
Men stand stiff, their handcuffs are gold
The one in the middle is crying
The man on the left is reading a sign
The last man is mad. They are sad and mad and hungry
The sad men.

    —Brittany Perry, fourth grade

The following two poems are about Lawrence paintings not in *The Great Migration* series. They show urban African Americans involved in community activities probably in the North. "The Library" is a bird's-eye view of a huge reading room:

The Library

Orange floor orange books orange
shirt. There are
many people in the library but
only one with a necklace.
All the people in the library
are reading books but
one is leaving. I am looking
out the window trying to figure
out my future.

    —Matthew Wilberg, fourth grade

Lawrence's "Community," on which the next poem is based, shows the hustle and bustle of a construction site:

So Many Things

Red boards, yellow boards,
purple ladder, black shoes,
brown hair, purple hat,
gray pants, so many people,

hands filled with newspapers,
or tools, people in corners, people
stomping, people humming a song,
smiling, laughing so hard
about to cry. Wearing a black hat
standing at the side, hearing loud
noises of pounding hammers and
saws. Happy, so very happy am I.

—*Ashley Horwath, fourth grade*

The following piece, based on an surreal, ironic painting entitled "Dreams," has a haunting quality similar to that of Hughes's poem:

Dreams

White gowns on black brides
red and pink flowers in their hands
brown hills, brown hills, brown hills forever.
Green walls and more green walls, trapping me inside.
Clear curtains blowing in the breeze,
making my dream come real.
Lying here, my dream is gone
and has left me all alone.

—*Genevieve Roudane, fourth grade*

Notes

1. Introduction, *The Great Migration: An American Story. Paintings by Jacob Lawrence.* New York: The Museum of Modern Art/The Phillips Collection/HarperCollins, 1993, unpaginated introduction.

2. "Jacob Lawrence: Twenty Notecards," reproducing Lawrence paintings from the collections of the National Museum of American Art, Smithsonian Institution, Washington, D.C., and published by Pomegranate Publications, Box 6099, Rohnert Park, California, 94927.

(Also available from The Museum of Modern Art, 11 West 53rd St., New York, NY 10019, are postcards of selected images from *The Great Migration*.)

Selected Bibliography and Other Resources

By Lorenzo Thomas

Anthologies of works by African American poets and writers were issued as early as the 1920s. Many of these collections have been periodically republished, while new anthologies—both textbooks and those intended for the general public—continue to appear. Among the most useful currently available titles are:

Adoff, Arnold, ed. *The Poetry of Black America.* New York: Harper & Row, 1973. An excellent selection of poems by 20th-century writers, including Owen Dodson, Gloria C. Oden, Julia Fields, and other fine poets who are often omitted from anthologies.

Cullen, Countee, ed. *Caroling Dusk: An Anthology of Verse by Black Poets of the Twenties.* 1927. New York: Citadel Press, 1993. Cullen focuses on poetry written in "the higher traditions of English verse." For example, he avoids Paul Laurence Dunbar's popular dialect poems in favor of lyrics such as the beautiful "Ere Sleep Come Down to Soothe the Weary Eyes."

Gates, Henry Louis, Jr., Nellie Y. McKay, and others, eds. *Norton Anthology of African American Literature.* New York: W. W. Norton, 1997. Valuable, thoroughly footnoted college text; includes audio CD that documents the African American oral tradition from spirituals and sermons to rap.

Harper, Michael S. and Anthony Walton, eds. *Every Shut Eye Ain't Asleep: An Anthology of Poetry by African Americans Since 1945.* Boston: Little, Brown, 1994. A good selection of works by well-known contemporary poets.

Hill, Patricia Liggins and others, eds. *Call and Response: The Riverside Anthology of the African American Literary Tradition.* Boston: Houghton Mifflin, 1998. An impressive college-level textbook. Selections demonstrate the relationship between traditional African art, folk art, and sophisticated literary forms. The introductory notes to selections are actually informative critical essays, and a CD of music and poetry performances is included.

Killens, John Oliver and Jerry W. Ward, Jr., eds. *Black Southern Voices: An Anthology of Fiction, Poetry, Drama, Nonfiction, and Critical Essays.* New York: Meridian/New American Library, 1992. Broad selection of works, from spirituals and Frederick Douglass to Albert Murray and Kalamu ya Salaam.

Major, Clarence, ed. *Calling the Wind: Twentieth-Century African-American Short Stories.* New York: Harper Perennial, 1993. Selections ranging from Charles W. Chesnutt (1899) to Terry McMillan.

———. *The Garden Thrives: Twentieth-Century African-American Poetry.* New York: Harper Perennial, 1996. Fine choices of work by major poets; includes several younger contemporary writers.

McMillan, Terry, ed. *Breaking Ice: An Anthology of Contemporary African-American Fiction.* New York: Penguin, 1990. Short stories and excerpts from recent novels.

Miller, E. Ethelbert, ed. *In Search of Color Everywhere: A Collection of African-American Poetry.* New York: Stewart, Tabori, and Chang, 1994. Illustrated by Terrance Cummings, this beautiful book includes work ranging from Phillis Wheatley to the rap group Public Enemy. The poems are arranged by theme.

Powell, Kevin and Ras Baraka, eds. *In the Tradition: An Anthology of Young Black Writers.* New York: Harlem River Press, 1992. Poetry and fiction from a new generation of militant black writers.

Randall, Dudley, ed. *The Black Poets.* New York: Bantam, 1971. This excellent, well-organized anthology has never gone out of print.

Rowell, Charles H., ed. *Ancestral House: The Black Short Story in the Americas and Europe.* New York: Westview Press, 1996. Stories from throughout the African diaspora.

Ward, Jerry W., Jr., ed. *Trouble the Water: 250 Years of African-American Poetry.* New York: Mentor, 1997. An excellent collection of works by more than 100 poets from 1746 to the 1990s.

Washington, Mary Helen, ed. *Black-Eyed Susans: Classic Stories by and about Black Women.* Garden City, New York: Anchor, 1975. Includes works by Alice Walker, Toni Cade Bambara, Louise Meriwether, and others; useful bibliographies. Appropriate for upper-level high school readers.

Wideman, Daniel J. and Rohan B. Preston, eds. *Soulfires: Young Black Men on Love and Violence.* New York: Penguin, 1996. Thoughtful, truthful, and powerfully candid writing on highly controversial topics. Includes poetry, fiction, and essays.

Young, Al, ed. *African American Literature: A Brief Introduction and Anthology.* New York: HarperCollins, 1996. A fine anthology of all genres of writing; part of the multicultural Literary Mosaic series under the general editorship of Ishmael Reed. Companion volumes present Hispanic, Asian American, and Native American literature.

Color: A Sampling of Contemporary African American Writers. VHS format videocassette, 57 minutes. 1994. Written and narrated by poet Al Young, this videotape anthology includes performances by twenty-two writers (Lucille Clifton, Rita Dove, Etheridge Knight, Lorenzo Thomas, among others) and a study guide with texts of poems and biographical notes. Available from The Poetry Center and American Poetry Archive, San Francisco State University, 1600 Holloway Avenue, San Francisco, CA 94132. Telephone (415) 338-1056.

> ▸   ▸   ▸

Many good works of reference and criticism are currently in print. Perhaps the most valuable for readers of this volume are:

Andrews, William L., Frances Smith Foster, and Trudier Harris, eds. *The Oxford Companion to African American Literature.* New York: Oxford University Press, 1997. This encyclopedic reference work includes biographies of authors, critical summaries of specific books, and general articles on relevant historical and literary topics.

Melhem, D. H. *Heroism in the New Black Poetry: Introductions and Interviews.* Lexington: University Press of Kentucky, 1990. Useful interviews with Amiri Baraka, Gwendolyn Brooks, Jayne Cortez, Dudley

Randall, and others focus on writing practices and literary influences. Melhem's wonderfully accessible critical introductions are appropriate for high school and college students.

, , ,

Excellent journals specifically devoted to African American literature and criticism include:

African American Review. Published quarterly; includes critical essays, poetry, fiction, and scholarly book reviews. Back issues (it began in 1967 as *Negro American Literature Forum*) can be found in most large university libraries and are also available on microfilm. Subscriptions available from the Department of English, Indiana State University, Terre Haute, IN 47809. Its web site—http://web.indstate.edu/artsci/ AAR—offers useful information.

The Black Scholar. Published quarterly; includes essays, poetry, book reviews. While mostly devoted to political and sociological concerns, at least one issue each year focuses on cultural history. Back issues are available on microfilm. Subscriptions available from P.O. Box 2869, Oakland, CA 94609.

Callaloo: A Journal of African-American and African Arts and Letters. Published quarterly; includes critical essays, interviews with writers, poetry, fiction, and book reviews. It focuses on literature of the entire hemisphere, with special issues on, for example, Afro-Brazilian fiction, contemporary Haitian poetry and fiction, and works by Puerto Rican women writers. Subscriptions are available from Johns Hopkins University Press, Journals Publishing Division, P.O. Box 19966, Baltimore, MD 21211. An on-line edition is available at http://muse.jhu.edu/journals/callaloo.

Drumvoices Revue: A Confluence of Literary, Cultural, and Vision Arts. Published twice a year; includes poetry, essays, and interviews with writers. Especially valuable for reports on writers' conferences in the United States and abroad. The editors are especially hospitable to new writers. Subscriptions available from the Department of English, Box 1431, Southern Illinois University, Edwardsville, IL 62026-1431.

Fertile Ground: An Annual Journal of Black Literature. Edited by Kalamu ya Salaam; includes poetry, fiction, and essays. Subscriptions available from Runagate Press, P.O. Box 52723, New Orleans, LA 70152-2723.

QBR: The Black Book Review. Published quarterly; includes feature articles, interviews with writers, reviews of current books. Excellent coverage of poetry books and books for children. Its nationwide directory of bookstores is frequently updated. Subscriptions available from QBR, 625 Broadway, 10th Floor, New York, NY 10012.

▸   ▸   ▸

Discography

The historical importance of the African American sermonic tradition and the nuances of the speaking voice—as noted in several of the essays in this book—makes *hearing* African American poets and writers a thrilling experience. Anthologies such as *Call and Response* and *Norton Anthology of African American Literature* include audio CDs. Also available on CD and audiocassette are:

An Anthology of African American Poetry for Young People. Smithsonian Institution/Folkways 45044. Arna Bontemps reads selections from many poets.

Anthology of Negro Poets. Smithsonian Institution/Folkways FL 9791. Edited by Arna Bontemps; includes Claude McKay, Countee Cullen, Langston Hughes, Margaret Walker, and others reading their own works.

Margaret Walker Reads. Smithsonian Institution/Folkways FL 9796.

The Poetry of Sterling A. Brown. Smithsonian Institution/Folkways 47002. Recordings by the poet, 1946–1973.

The Voice of Langston Hughes. Smithsonian Institution/Folkways 47001. Recordings of poetry from the 1950s and other narratives including Hughes's *The Story of Jazz.*

The Folkways Records collection of more than 2,000 albums is housed at Cultural Studies, 955 L'Enfant Plaza, Suite 2600 MRC 914, Washington, D.C. 20560. Internet users can address http://www.si.edu/folkways

for on-line information. Everything in the catalogue is available on audiocassette by special order.

The works of many contemporary poets—usually in collaboration
with musicians—are also available on CD. Among recent releases are
works by Jayne Cortez, Nathaniel Mackey, Kalamu ya Salaam, Sekou
Sundiata, and Quincy Troupe. Such CDs are usually found in the "Spoken Word" section of large record stores.

Notes on Contributors

OPAL PALMER ADISA, born in Jamaica, is a literary critic, writer, and storyteller. Her five books include *It Begins with Tears*, a novel, and *Tamarind and Mango Women*, a collection of poems that received the PEN Oakland/Josephine Miles Award. Her poems, children's poems, and essays have been widely anthologized. With a Ph.D. in Ethnic Studies Literature, Adisa is Associate Professor and Chair of the Ethnic Studies/Cultural Diversity Program at California College of Arts and Crafts. She lives in Oakland, California.

KENT ALEXANDER, the author of several nonfiction books, is also a playwright and fiction writer. Through Teachers & Writers Collaborative and other organizations, since 1991 he has conducted award-winning theater and fiction workshops in the New York City schools and hospitals. Since 1994 he has served as a keynote speaker for the Columbia Scholarship Press Association's annual fall and spring conferences.

CATHERINE BARNETT has worked as a senior editor and staff writer for *Art & Antiques* magazine and *Martha Stewart Living*. Her articles have appeared in national and international publications such as *Mirabella, Sports Illustrated, House & Garden, Travel & Leisure,* and *New York Newsday*. She teaches with Teachers & Writers Collaborative and with the Children's Museum of Manhattan, where she leads writing workshops for teen mothers. She is at work on a collection of poems.

Through the Bronx WritersCorp program, ILISE BENUN teaches creative writing to children and adults at the Edenwald-Gun Hill Neighborhood Center in the Bronx, N.Y. She also teaches at the Calabro Primary School in Hoboken, N.J. In 1994 she was awarded a Prose Fellowship by the New Jersey State Council on the Arts.

MELBA BOYD is the author of five books of poetry, the most recent of which are *Letters to Che* and *The Inventory of Black Roses*. She is also the author of a bio-critical study, *Discarded Legacy: Politics and Poetics in the Life of Frances E. W. Harper*. She has given lectures and poetry readings throughout the U.S. and Europe. In 1983–84 she was a Senior

Fulbright Lecturer at the University of Bremen (Germany). Boyd received her Doctor of Arts degree in English from the University of Michigan–Ann Arbor and has taught at the University of Iowa, Ohio State University, and the University of Michigan-Flint. She is currently an associate professor and the chair of the Department of Africana Studies Program at Wayne State University.

Since 1991, RENÉE-NOELLE FELICE has received three grants from the New York City Department of Cultural Affairs. She has read and performed at colleges, libraries, and houses of worship in Staten Island, N.Y., and has been poet-in-residence at public schools in all five boroughs of New York City.

MARGOT FORTUNATO GALT is a poet who has taught imaginative writing at all levels. She received a Ph.D. in American Studies from the University of Minnesota. In 1992, Teachers & Writers published her book *The Story in History: Writing Your Way into the American Experience.* She is also a contributor to T&W's *Old Faithful: 18 Writers Present Their Favorite Writing Assignments* and *The Teachers & Writers Guide to Frederick Douglass.* Her collection of poems is entitled *The Country's Way with Rain* (Kutenai Press). Galt teaches at Hamline University in St. Paul, Minnesota.

PEGGY GARRISON received an M.A. in creative writing from The City University of New York. She has been teaching poetry in public schools since 1976. She also teaches creative writing at New York University. In 1993 Garrison received the New York City Arts in Education Roundtable Award for Sustained Achievement in Literature. Her poetry, fiction, and essays have appeared in *The Literary Review, Beloit Fiction Journal, Teachers & Writers, The Village Voice, Poetry New York,* and many other magazines.

AURELIA LUCÍA HENRIQUEZ teaches in the Brentwood School District in Long Island, N.Y. Of both Native American and Puerto Rican heritage, Henriquez integrates the culture and literature of Native Americans, Latinos, and African Americans into the everyday curriculum. Her particular interest is in the relationships between the

African slaves and the peoples indigenous to Long Island and the Caribbean.

PATRICIA SPEARS JONES is the author of two collections of poetry, *Mythologizing Always* and *The Weather That Kills*. Her poems have appeared in many anthologies and magazines. She has read her work and taught writing workshops at The University of Kansas, The Poetry Project, The Nuyorican Poets Cafe, Barnard College, and the Studio Museum in Harlem. Jones is the recipient of grants from the Foundation for Contemporary Performance Arts, the N.Y. Foundation for the Arts, and the National Endowment for the Arts.

PHILLIP LOPATE is the author of *Portrait of My Body, Against Joie de Vivre, Bachelorhood, The Rug Merchant, Being with Children,* and *Confessions of Summer.* His works have appeared in *Best American Essays, The Paris Review,* Pushcart Prize annuals, and many other publications. Also, Lopate edited the definitive anthology, *The Art of the Personal Essay.* In 1997 he was appointed editor of *Anchor Annual Essays,* a best-of-each-year collection. A recipient of Guggenheim and National Endowment for the Arts fellowships, he lives in New York City and is Adams Professor of English at Hofstra University.

JANICE LOWE is a writer and composer. Her one act-plays have been performed in Absolute Theatre's "Urban Fairy Tale Festival" in Manhattan. She has composed music for five plays, including two avantgarde productions of Shakespeare. Her poems have appeared in magazines and anthologies. Lowe lives in New York City, where she facilitates poetry and folktale writing by young people.

MICHAEL MORSE has an M.F.A. in poetry from the Iowa Writers' Workshop and currently teaches English at the Ethical Culture Fieldston School and poetry classes for the Gotham Writers' Workshop. He has taught poetry in the schools for Teachers & Writers Collaborative, as well as undergraduate courses at The University of Iowa and The City University of New York. His poems have been published in *The Colorado Review, Iowa Review, Antioch Review,* and *Field.*

RON PADGETT is the editor of *The Teachers & Writers Handbook of Poetic Forms*, as well as other volumes on teaching writing. His own books include *New & Selected Poems, Creative Reading: What It Is, How to Do It, and Why*, and a translation of *The Complete Poems of Blaise Cendrars*. Padgett is the recipient of a Guggenheim Fellowship, a Fulbright Fellowship, and a grants from the New York State Council on the Arts and the National Endowment for the Arts. In addition to serving as T&W's publications director, Padgett teaches Imaginative Writing at Columbia University.

JULIE PATTON, the recipient of the New York City Roundtable Award for Sustained Achievement in Arts Education and the Touchstone Fellowship Award for Teaching Artists, has served as an arts consultant to public schools since 1976, working primarily through Teachers & Writers Collaborative. She has also taught at the Naropa Institute (Colorado), the Schule für Dichtung (Austria), the Universitie Antiochita (Colombia), and the Westfalische Literaturburo (Germany). Patton's artistic activities span poetry, performance, and the visual arts. Her collection of poetry is *Teething on Type* (Rodent Press). Her essay is an excerpt from a work in progress entitled *The Mark of Cane*.

ELIZABETH RABY is a poet who works as a writer-in-the-schools for the New Jersey Council of the Arts. One of her essays, about using Native American sources to inspire student writing, appeared in *Old Faithful* (Teachers & Writers). Her own books include *The Hard Scent of Peonies* (Jasper Press) and *Camphorwood* (Nightshade Press).

LEN ROBERTS, the author of seven books of poetry, translations from Hungarian, and an autobiography, has been teaching poetry writing for more than twenty years. His *Black Wings* was selected for the National Poetry Series, and he has received a Guggenheim Fellowship in Poetry and two grants from the National Endowment for the Arts. His most recent book is *The Trouble-Making Finch*. Roberts lives in Hellertown, Pennsylvania, with his wife and son.

MARK STATMAN's writing has appeared in a number of journals, including *notus, Transfer, The Village Voice, The Nation, Democracy & Education,* and *The Pacific Review,* as well as in book collections such as *Luna, Luna; Old Faithful; The Teachers & Writers Guide to Walt Whitman;* and *The Teachers & Writers Handbook of Poetic Forms.* He has received grants from the National Endowment for the Arts and the National Writing Project, and was the recipient of the Columbia Press Association's Gold Key. Since 1985 Statman has taught writing for Teachers & Writers Collaborative and at Eugene Lang College at the New School for Social Research.

LORENZO THOMAS, the editor of this volume, is Associate Professor of English at the University of Houston-Downtown, where he teaches American Literature and Creative Writing and serves as Director of the Cultural Enrichment Center. Thomas is a widely published poet and critic whose works have appeared in many journals, as well as in reference books such as *The Oxford Companion to African American Literature* and *Encyclopedia of African-American Culture and History.* His own collections of poetry include *Chances Are Few, The Bathers,* and *There Are Witnesses.* He has read and performed his work at venues across the U.S. and Europe.

SUSAN MARIE SWANSON is a poet who has taught in the COMPAS Writers and Artists in the Schools program in Minnesota since 1983. In the summer, she teaches at Summit Arts, a program for young children at St. Paul Academy. Her books include a collection of poems for children, *Getting Used to the Dark,* and a picture book, *Letter to the Lake.*

OTHER T&W BOOKS YOU MIGHT ENJOY

The T&W Guide to Frederick Douglass edited by Wesley Brown provides a variety of ways for students to experience Douglass' *Narrative* as an aesthetic achievement as well as a socio-historical document. "An impressive collection, well written . . . solid and very usable . . . particularly inspiring"—*Contemporary Education.*

Luna, Luna: Creative Writing Ideas from Spanish, Latin American, & Latino Literature, edited by Julio Marzán. In 21 lively and practical essays, poets, fiction writers, and teachers tell how they used the work of Lorca, Neruda, Jiménez, Cisneros, and others to inspire students to write imaginatively. *Luna, Luna* "succeeds brilliantly. I highly recommend this book: it not only teaches but guides teachers on how to involve students in the act of creative writing"—*Kliatt.*

The Teachers & Writers Handbook of Poetic Forms, edited by Ron Padgett. This T&W bestseller includes 74 entries on traditional and modern poetic forms by 19 poet-teachers. "A treasure"—*Kliatt.* "The definitions not only inform, they often provoke and inspire. A small wonder!"—*Poetry Project Newsletter.* "An entertaining reference work"—*Teaching English in the Two-Year College.* "A solid beginning reference source"—*Choice.*

The Story in History: Writing Your Way into the American Experience by Margot Fortunato Galt. "One of the best idea books for teachers I have ever read. . . . Rich lodes of writing ideas. . . . This is a book that can make a difference"—*Kliatt.*

Poetry Everywhere: Teaching Poetry Writing in School and in the Community by Jack Collom & Sheryl Noethe. This big and "tremendously valuable resource work for teachers" (*Kliatt*) at all levels contains 60 writing exercises, extensive commentary, and 450 examples.

The T&W Guide to Walt Whitman edited by Ron Padgett. The first and only guide to teaching the work of Walt Whitman from K–college. "A lively, fun, illuminating book"—Ed Folsom, editor of *The Walt Whitman Quarterly.*

Educating the Imagination, Vols. 1 & 2, edited by Christopher Edgar and Ron Padgett. A huge selection of the best articles from 17 years of *Teachers & Writers* magazine, with ideas and assignments for writing poetry, fiction, plays, history, folklore, parodies, and much more.

Old Faithful: 18 Writers Present Their Favorite Writing Assignments, edited by Christopher Edgar and Ron Padgett. A collection of sure-fire exercises in imaginative writing for all levels, developed and tested by veteran writing teachers.

▶   ▶   ▶

For a complete free T&W publications catalogue, contact
Teachers & Writers Collaborative
5 Union Square West, New York, NY 10003–3306
tel. (toll-free) 888-BOOKS-TW
Visit our World Wide Web site at http://www.twc.org